MANUAL NOT INCLUDED

HILARIA BALDWIN

GALLERY BOOKS

New York Amsterdam/Antwerp London
Toronto Sydney/Melbourne New Delhi

G

Gallery Books

An Imprint of Simon & Schuster, LLC

1230 Avenue of the Americas

New York, NY 10020

First Gallery Books hardcover edition May 2025

GALLERY BOOKS and colophon are registered trademarks of Simon & Schuster, LLC

Simon & Schuster strongly believes in freedom of expression and stands against censorship in all its forms. For more information, visit BooksBelong.com.

For information about special discounts for bulk purchases, please contact Simon & Schuster Special Sales at 1-866-506-1949 or business@simonandschuster.com.

The Simon & Schuster Speakers Bureau can bring authors to your live event. For more information or to book an event, contact the Simon & Schuster Speakers Bureau at 1-866-248-3049 or visit our website at www.simonspeakers.com.

INTERIOR DESIGN BY KARLA SCHWEER

Manufactured in the United States of America

1   3   5   7   9   10   8   6   4   2

Library of Congress Cataloging-in-Publication Data is available.

ISBN 978-1-6680-0998-7

ISBN 978-1-6680-1000-6 (ebook)

For anyone who wants
to tell their own story.

✳

CONTENTS

INTRODUCTION

Looking back on my life over the past fifteen years or so, I realized that I often felt obligated to defend or explain things about myself: Why did I marry somebody so much older? Why was I making a certain parenting choice? Why did I have so many children? I was constantly on edge, trying to prove that I wasn't a gold digger, out of touch, or fake—nor was I practicing any nefarious witchery. Through many tears, insight from others, hard work and growth, I have learned that none of those outside opinions had anything to do with me. I don't blame those who gossip; I feel for them, because they are a product of a system that most of us play into. We fear that if we question the system, we will get hurt and be ostracized. What if we stop telling ourselves that there is some limit on what we're capable of? It's all made-up. What if we switch the way that we function, take the targets off, the weighted opinions, and through kindness, community, and wisdom, we march on, together?

This book is not about me preaching or telling anyone what to do. Far from it. It's about admitting that this womaning and mothering and partnering and life-ing thing is hard. There is no step-by-step guidebook for how to successfully tackle every difficult situation we come across in our lives. At a certain point we have to come to the frightening and empowering realization that we are the adults in the room, the parenting CEOs, the ones who have to take a deep breath and make choices that affect our families and our lives. No one else is living our lives. We will undoubtedly get some things wrong and hopefully more things right, but the goal I strive for is to lead my life with care, humor, resourcefulness, and love as best I can.

Throughout these chapters I will share personal stories, snippets, and vignettes within the common themes that unite many of us. The ups, the downs, the ways I've handled challenges and experienced joy, and how I've processed heartbreak and attempts to move forward. It is through hearing stories from other women and mothers that I myself grow and learn and navigate life. Take it for what you will. Because, as it says on the cover of this book: MANUAL NOT INCLUDED!

1

—

NOT A CINDERELLA STORY

As humans, we try to hold on to people, to control them, and we're afraid to allow them to change. It comes down to the simplest desire: Do we both want to be here, and do we want to make it work?

I have been through amazing times together with my husband, Alec: having kids, experiencing great joy, meeting fascinating people, and being able to see incredible things. And we've also had hard moments that have been extremely painful. Through it all, we've chosen to stick together and grow together.

I believe that some parts of relationships are about growing and equal parts are about letting go. Letting go of our egos.

Letting go of our expectations for the perfect partner. Letting go of the idea of keeping score. When we let go, we have space to move on to new and good things. Relationships can be such hard work, including my relationship with Alec. Like many, we have fought through the darkest times, wanting to quit, wanting to walk away, and we somehow found our way back to a happy and good place. Scars, memories, lessons, exhaustion—all come with that package of staying together. We do this so that all the beauty and fulfillment of a good relationship can bring us happiness.

Stepping into Alec's life meant being presented to this world as a supporting character. We have been riddled with fairy tales our whole lives, and when we are familiar with someone, often we cannot help but see their love interest through this lens. I love a fairy tale, but I hate the idea that Alec somehow chose me like Prince Charming chose Cinderella. I was a whole person before I met him, with autonomy, and I lived happily and was constantly evolving. I existed before Alec and I had agency in saying yes to going out with him on our first date. We continued to date, spent time getting to know each other, and chose a life together. This is our story.

✳

When Alec and I met, I was twenty-seven and he was fifty-three. Now, it's nearly a decade and a half later. Our generations—boomer and millennial—feel like different cultures, but neither is better or smarter than the other. I think there is a tendency for humans to reject the old and think that our contemporary world is the most evolved. It is probably why we constantly strive to grow and invent and change. How humbling it is to think that we all just exist in a moment in time and what is ours and new will soon become old.

For the first six weeks that we dated, Alec just wanted to talk. He would shake my hand hello and goodbye. Sometimes these early conversations were intense: he told me how much he liked me, that he could see a future with me, and he wanted to know if I was open to having children. I found his directness fascinating and funny and odd. As much as I found humor in his old-fashioned dating style, I also found it refreshing and completely different from what I was used to. I was like, *What is this?* He wanted to get to know me and this allowed me not to feel pressured and to get to know him too. It wasn't

Marco Vacchi

purely about physical attraction; it was true respect. No one had ever wanted to get to know me in quite that way before.

I'd never dated anyone so much older than me. I ended up loving that he was at a point in his life where he knew his intentions, what he wanted out of a relationship, and that he could express this to me. I could relax and let go of that eternal dating fear: *Does he like me? Will he call me back?* I didn't have to wonder with Alec. He made it clear and he showed up. I allowed myself to let go of my insecurity—let go of my fear of heartbreak and the uncertainty of the future. I leaned in. We both did. People often look at our age difference as weird or a negative—sometimes we do too!—but I feel that one of the huge benefits is that the older we get, the more we are aware of how precious life is.

Marrying a man with a public profile, about whom people have strong opinions and who is seen as an "eligible bachelor," is wading into bumpy territory—good and bad. I filmed an episode of *Love Ride* with Alec once. It was this cute show about couples' advice where Alec would drive around Manhattan with a comedian and chat with couples who agreed to be interviewed for the show. For the episode that I was in, I entered the car and the couple didn't know who I was or that I was married to Alec. We were talking about celebrity crushes, and the woman said that Alec would be the celebrity she would most like to "boff." I asked her why he was the celebrity she'd like to sleep with, and she had this whole imagined scene of him pouring champagne down her back; it felt very Jack Donaghy, wild and exciting. I had to inform her that she should probably choose a different famous man to fantasize about, because Alec is nothing like that. Alec has been sober for forty years, so wild champagne nights are not in his repertoire.

Most of the time, I joke about the idea that my husband has been (and still is), for some people, a fantasy of someone they'd like to be with. What's not funny is the cruelty from the tabloid media and online trolls who try to diminish me, labeling me as a gold-digging younger woman, someone who doesn't deserve to be with him. Or I must be some kind of temptress who tricked him into marrying me. I never took gold-digging classes and I definitely don't have a diploma from Temptress U. I have given a lot of thought to why people want to try to label me as such, because I've lived with these attacks for a while now. Here's my theory, please bear with me: if you are a successful gold digger, you have one kid, spend a few years with your husband, then get out of the marriage and take his money. We have seen it modeled. I can tell you that seven kids shouldn't be in the gold-digging curriculum, and I would probably receive a solid D– for this choice. Kids are expensive and a lot of hard work. Gold diggers want maximum money and minimal responsibility.

All kidding aside, I have gotten to a point in my life where I feel that sometimes we are much less evolved than we would like to admit. Our animal instincts are part of what draws us to a partner, and it is often for comfort, resources, and shelter. Alec was seen by many as a well and I had the audacity to jump the line and drink from it. But I want nothing to do with the idea that I was "chosen." Alec isn't some prize, and I often kid that anyone who wants to take him off my hands is welcome to. I guarantee, you'll send him back in half an hour, express.

When I was presented to the world as Alec's girlfriend fourteen years ago, there were jokes about my age and my profession. I mean, I can laugh along with that as well: What's more cliché than an older man dating a twenty-seven-year-old yoga instructor? But after a few laughs, it would have been nice to come back to the reality that the person was me: a real human, with a real job, at which I worked very hard and in which I took much pride.

No matter who dated Alec Baldwin, she was going to be picked apart. We've all seen the articles dissecting the newest love interest of whatever celebrity, and there was nothing truly unique about the stories written about us—just the fine details. I am constantly practicing tuning out opinions that have nothing to do with me. (I speak about how I do this in my first book, *The Living Clearly Method*.) The gist is that when negativity starts to seep in, I try to notice it, breathe, ground myself, balance, redirect, and let it go. It is a practice that will never lead to perfection, but it helps to guide me back to reality. When I am having a hard moment, my mother always asks me: "Is this a problem with Hilaria or is it a problem with Hilaria Baldwin?" Separating me from the character random people talk about—people who don't actually know me—is helpful for protecting my mental health. We all have people in our lives who don't really know us but judge us anyway. I highly recommend separating your true self from the caricature created from gossip. Think about it in your own life. Do certain people characterize you and think of you differently than someone else's description? If we base our self-worth on the opinions of others, we lose ourselves.

One of the fascinating things about living in Public-Figure-Landia is that you can be known as two totally opposite things at the exact same time. You can be brilliant and evil: just click on two different stories written by two different people. You can be too fat and too skinny—both at once! You can be an amazing mother—one who was either pregnant or breastfeeding for over a decade—or a childless woman who wears fake bellies. (Yes, trolls have actually written the latter about me.) While there have been jokes about my and Alec's age difference, my profession, and the big difference in our incomes, I have also been depicted as some sort of savior for Alec. To recap: I am both a gold-digging temptress and a healthy, positive influence—at the same time. Sometimes I've wondered: *What would it take to prove that I am in this for the right reasons?* For those who do not want to see our reality, the answer is: absolutely nothing. They don't want to see the truth; they want to get riled up about a fantasy. Rather than sit around and be sad and feel like a victim, I practice getting up, filtering it all out, and living my own best life, secure in the knowledge that those people are full of it. It is our empathetic and sweet selves that want to be understood and embraced. There are so many positive people to lean on—more than the negative people who want to tear others down. I focus my energies on the positive ones and it feels good.

Before I met Alec, he had a reputation for being rough around the edges, a fiery person who didn't take care of his stress or his health. He got healthier when he started dating me and seemed happy. He spoke a lot about this, for which he and the press both gave me misplaced credit. I can never take credit for someone else's choices and hard work to get healthier and happier. We can make suggestions and try to be good partners, but it is the individual who makes the changes and chooses how to live; no one can force someone to change or do it for them. I will never accept credit for anyone else's hard work.

At one point early in our relationship, we were in the Hamptons, taking a walk on the beach, when Alec got a phone call from his doctor. We sat down on a big piece of driftwood and he spoke with his doctor in a serious tone. After he hung up, he was visibly upset. The doctor had said Alec's blood work showed that he was prediabetic. This is a very upsetting thing for anyone to hear. I just let him know that I was there if he wanted me to be.

Through my work, I had experience helping yoga students with both their physical and emotional health issues. I knew that if Alec tried, he could get his health to a place where he'd start to feel better.

"It's going to be okay," I said. "You can positively impact your blood sugar level by changing your diet. I know it feels overwhelming, and even though the answer is simple, humans are creatures of habit and change is hard. It is simple and it's hard. But I can help you if you want me to. We can do this together." I made lists of foods to eat and not to eat. I packed lunches that he would bring to the *30 Rock* set at NBC. His costar and the show's creator, Tina Fey, found this very amusing. She would range between lightheartedly teasing "Did your mommy pack your lunch?" and "I want my own Hilaria!"—which I found funny. Steadily, Alec's body healed and he started to feel much better.

As I noted above, changing one's diet or fitness regimen isn't something to force on someone. They have to make their own choices that feel right for their life and body, and most importantly, they have to do it. Alec committed to healthier eating. He made that choice: it wasn't me. I was a good partner to him—I never shamed him, only encouraged him.

By being by Alec's side while he was noticeably taking care of himself, I was seen as softening the image of a once—as depicted by the media, of course—hothead, bad dad, and horrible husband. I can tell you that he is none of these things. So many people embraced us in Alec's personal, professional, and public lives. I can hold him and support him in good times and hard times, but he makes his own life choices, just like I do.

※

Alec and I had been dating for a year when we celebrated our first Valentine's Day. I very much identify as a Capricorn: up for a challenge, disciplined, hardworking, practical. In other words, I'm not a typical romantic. My love language is acts of service: I'm very caring and I want to make sure you feel good. But I'm not going to buy you a pink card and gush over you. My love isn't any less or more; I just show it differently than some.

That day, Alec had asked if I was a Valentine's Day person. I told him I wasn't, and since we were both working late, I assumed we were off the hook. End of conversation.

Around 8:00 p.m., he picked me up at the yoga studio I was working at and said, "I've made a reservation, and I'm not going to tell you where."

It turned out it was a restaurant downtown. We were eating and having a fun time when he pulled out a valentine. I'm not good at getting cards: I don't like being watched while I read them. It makes me uncomfortable. I read it, gave him a quick kiss, and returned to my dinner.

"Where's *my* card?" he asked, smiling at me expectantly.

"I thought we weren't Valentine's Day people. I don't have one."

"That's funny," he said. "No, really, where's my card?"

"I thought we had a conversation about this. We said we weren't doing that."

Then he said, "Don't worry, I have an extra card in my bag. When we get home, you can fill it out for me."

Wait. What?

Back home, Alec handed me the card. I couldn't believe he was serious. On the one hand, I felt like I'd let him down. On the other hand, I knew I was totally in the right! We'd said we weren't doing anything. At that moment I was getting a lot of information about my boyfriend. It was a real look into Alec Baldwin. He's romantic, he's emotional—even needy at times. He tells you exactly what it is that he needs and exactly when he needs it. I was also going to tell him exactly what I felt: that signing his card on demand didn't feel authentic to me. So, in my usual way, I refused to do it.

The next day, as I talked with my friends about what had happened the night before, we laughed at what a disaster I was when it came to sappy romance, especially compared to Alec's amorous and often over-the-top gestures. Leaning into humor after a fight felt like a good tactic to use with a funny actor. So my friends and I cooked up a plan and headed to a store a few blocks away and bought the most ridiculous, cheesy Valentine's Day cards and decorations at 75 percent off. We then molded hearts and flowers out of Play-Doh and construction paper and made a trail of the hearts from the front door to the bedroom. Then we decorated the room with all the leftover February 14 junk that no one wanted to buy. It looked like Valentine's Day had vomited all over our bedroom! I was sure Alec would think it was so funny.

When Alec got home, he followed the trail and found me waiting for him in the bedroom. I expected a big laugh to erupt, but instead he started tearing up and said, "This is so beautiful."

How could this be? Mind racing, I started feeling even more awkward than the night before. By making fun of what I thought were silly gestures, I'd stumbled onto what he really wanted, which was the Hallmark version of romance. Clearly, I had a lot to learn about this man, what he needed, and what mattered to him.

In the years since that first Valentine's Day fiasco, I've discovered that Alec often buys two cards for most special occasions, then chooses the one that best matches his sentiment for the person on that day. He leads strongly by feeling, which is why I think so many are drawn to him. He is messy and raw and wears his heart on his sleeve.

Now, no matter the occasion, I make sure to always get Alec a card—not because he forces me to or guilts me into it, but simply because I know how much it means to him. It is an exercise in mushy romance that I struggle with, but I try and try again, even when the words on my card don't flow as well as his. My trying is part of how I show my love for him. I try to let go of my shyness and make room to grow.

And while I do want my expression of my romantic feelings to be authentic, I do think Alec has taught me to soften a little bit and that it's not weak to show emotion or be vulnerable. Rather, it's courageous to do so. I saw a quote on a Manhattan garden box the other day: "In memory of Joe, who had the courage to be a romantic." How true.

I don't remember a specific conversation in which Alec and I decided to get married. It felt right, and it always just was, stemming from the fact that we spent tons of time together and talked and talked and talked.

He was very focused on getting me an engagement ring. In the beginning, I was like, "I don't need a ring!" My mom doesn't have an engagement ring, and it wasn't something I felt strongly about. (Now we joke about this because I've changed my ring twice. Once I had a taste, I quickly got on the ring train!) Alec sent me to Cartier to pick a ring out. In typical me fashion, I showed up with two girlfriends and we said all the embarrassing and cringey things that one should never say in

Cartier. They graciously served us champagne and sparkling water and little mints with their logo on them—the simple things that made our out-of-place selves excited! It didn't take much to impress us. To be honest, I wasn't familiar with the store because Audrey Hepburn didn't have breakfast at Cartier. Saleah, the salesperson, who is now my friend, greeted me and had me look at rings. She seemed clearly disappointed by my lack of diamond knowledge. I had googled a random photo of an engagement ring, screenshotted probably the first one to come up, and, when asked what I was looking for, awkwardly showed her the image on my phone. Saleah quickly and calmly stated, "No, this is not what you like." She's very Obi-Wan Kenobi. She showed me only one ring and, with her Jedi mind tricks, told me that it was what I liked. It was beautiful and simple, but I didn't like it. But how to tell her this? I mean, who says no to a diamond ring at Cartier when you didn't even want a ring in the first place? I was polite and simply agreed. Ultimate sign of a people pleaser.

I was asked recently why Alec didn't come with me to pick out the ring (or pick one out himself). This actually never occurred to me, so when I asked him, he told me that he wanted me to have the ring I wanted and felt I could choose one with my girlfriends. Alec was excited when he finally had it in hand and told me immediately. (He's terrible at keeping secrets from me: anytime he's thrown me a surprise party, I've known about it beforehand.) That weekend we were going to go out to the Hamptons and Alec said, "Make sure you don't forget to tell me to bring the ring." This ridiculousness is so us. Of course, we ended up forgetting the ring at home, so we had to drive back to the apartment to get it. Even more classic us: we're always just bumbling through life. Watching the two of us try to do anything, most people would look at us, head askew, and be like, *Why do they do things that way?* Great question.

That was a Friday night. Then, on Saturday morning, Alec said matter-of-factly, "You're going to go and do *your* workout, and I'm going to go do *my* workout. Then we'll meet at Babette's for lunch, and then I'm going to bring you somewhere to get engaged." And I was like, "Okay!" He cracked me up with his regimental way of organizing everything. Always narrating the schedule of the day.

It was a cold and dreary spring day, and we drove out to Montauk, which is at the very end of Long Island, the easternmost point of New York State. My family lives in Spain, so this was Alec's romantic idea: it was the closest he could get to my family while he was asking me to marry him.

We ended up at the Montauk Point Lighthouse, and to get out of the cold and the rain we went inside the little museum there. I'd never been to that quirky little place. There was a life-size sea captain doll in one room, and Alec thought that would be a good spot to get engaged, even though there were tourists everywhere. While I have made it clear I am not a typical romantic, even I thought: *Is he going to get down on one knee in this random museum and ask me to marry him?* Yes, yes he was.

"I think I'm going to do it here!" he said.

"No! I don't want to get engaged next to this life-size sea captain doll."

Due to the museum visitors and the small rooms, we couldn't find a private place, so we ventured outside. Alec tried to make me sit on a soaked bench. (Alec likes to orchestrate things; I think it's the actor/director in him.) I didn't want to get my butt wet, so I said no. It was cold, and I hate being cold. We awkwardly continued to wander around and eventually he just got down on his knee and asked me to marry him, and of course I said yes. We hugged and we kissed and he placed the ring on my finger. I've seen many engagement moments when it's this huge surprise, and it's so beautiful, but that's not us. I probably would have felt totally awkward. This wasn't a spontaneous thing; it was the opposite, which is very much who we are as a couple. And it was reflective of our quirky

nature. When things feel right—when they feel like "us"—we act on them and just do them.

The only other person nearby was a teenage girl. Alec said to her, "We're going to tell you a secret: we just got engaged. Don't tell anyone! Will you take a picture?" And she took the pictures that we now have, commemorating the experience. I often wonder if she knew who Alec was or if she just thought we were some weird and very wet adults.

I was so excited on the drive home, and when we got back, I immediately went upstairs to call my friends and family and send pictures of the ring. I headed into the bathroom to talk because Alec likes to keep the house cold and I like it hot, and the bathroom had its own thermostat, so I would crank it up and hang out in there. Alec stayed downstairs, and suddenly I heard him start screaming with total urgency and fear in his voice. "Get down on the ground: she's here!" I'd never heard him sound like that before. I threw myself to the ground, heart pumping, so confused. Who was here? He yelled up again: "She's at the door! I'm calling the police." He was referring to the woman who had been stalking and harassing us.

The police came, but she'd gotten away. They couldn't find her. I don't want to talk much about her here. She was and still is a very terrifying person to me. She intruded into our lives over and over, and for this she was eventually sent to Rikers Island. It was very scary and very sad.

That night, Alec wanted to go out to dinner and celebrate our engagement, and we did, but I was miserable, terrified that this woman would show up again at any moment. I made

Alec turn on every light before we went to sleep. Having been in the public eye for so many years, Alec has learned how to continue on when someone invades our space. While it isn't right for someone to do this, I had to develop a filter to not obsess about this all the time. I am still working on it, changing focus. It's upsetting, but to dwell on it is to lose my mind.

✳

Alec and I moved in together really fast. When I asked my mother if she thought it was too fast, she said, "It's either too fast or just right! Time will tell." Even though I never slept there again, I did keep my studio apartment, until the day before we got married. I wanted to have a backup, in case it *was* actually too fast, and not just right! A couple of days before our wedding, some friends of mine and I went to my apartment and packed everything up. I guess this was my major leap of going all in.

A few months after we met, Alec purchased an apartment for us to live in together. While this place was new for both of us, I also moved into his house in Amagansett, on Long Island. Moving into a partner's home is a topic I hear tons of couples talk about. Decorating, dealing with the other person's stuff, the difficulty with change . . . it can all present some challenges.

Alec always said to me, "I don't want you to feel like a guest here; I want you to feel welcome. This is your house too." But it was one thing for him to say these things and another when it came down to the actual changes that someone else living there would bring. I quickly learned that Alec was very particular and set in his ways. He was used to having things be a certain way. He found comfort in sameness, and that brought a sense of stability into his life. Because of this, I was very cautious about making any changes, and I had a hard time treating his home as mine. I had a few drawers for my things, and then eventually part of the closet. I put a picture of me holding my nephew when he was a baby by my bedside. Alec wanted these things in theory, but the small changes definitely pushed at his comfort level.

When we got married, I decided I was going to get more focused on making the house "ours." I began with the pantry. Odd, I know, but it felt like the most reasonable place to begin, because he had things in there that were expired—like for a decade or almost two. We ate every meal out at this point, so the pantry wasn't a place that got much attention, and I figured it had just been forgotten. There was everything from jelly to canned goods to chips and crackers in there, probably remnants of lots of gift baskets given to him over the years, I thought. Throw all these things out? It was a no-brainer.

I told him I was going to tackle the pantry as he headed out one day. He seemed fine with it, only asking that I throw things out in the precise way he likes. Yes, Alec is *very* meticulous about how to dispose of things. On one hand, this is great, because he tries to be environmentally conscious. On the other hand, some of his "rules" make zero sense. For example, we used to have a high grass patch outside our home that he would "compost" food in. I didn't know much about composting back then, but I do now! And throwing food in the grass isn't composting; it's just throwing food in the grass. I was skeptical, but I went with it.

As you might imagine, the smell of expired food is ... bad. I had to open all these cans and jars and walk outside with each individual one and pour it out, then rinse it all and recycle it properly.

I'm not a big drinker, particularly in the daytime, but in an attempt to deal with the stench, I opened a bottle of wine that afternoon. I spent the day reading expiration dates, opening cans and jars and then emptying and rinsing them, and then drinking. I don't know if alcohol helped, but I made it through, and when Alec came home, I had the shelves all cleared, with only probably about three remaining products.

I wasn't prepared for how upset this made him, and I didn't understand him well enough at this point to grasp that this was his OCD manifesting. He's very particular about his things, and sometimes he kind of hoards stuff, and everything has to be just so.

So he was mad. And I was mad, since I had just dealt with something so gross, and done it in the weird way he had insisted on. Of course we got over it, but that experience was a crash course in Alec and his OCD. Over the years, we have learned how the other one thinks and will react to certain situations. When we understand each other, we can grow and approach the other in ways that will hopefully not result in fighting. We can be empathetic and understanding and not have to tiptoe around each other, getting done what needs to be done and also accomplishing what we want.

We now cook at home all the time, which was a big deal for him. He doesn't like the lingering smell of food, so he has had to practice deep breathing and sitting with things that feel a little bit uncomfortable. He also came to realize that home-cooked food is literally the best. Major win.

Does he still go check the trash to make sure everything is the way he feels it needs to be? Yes. At the same time, we don't have to stress out about stacking the recycling the exact way he wants us to.

Our balanced relationship is not just my learning the way that Alec thinks; it's also his learning how I think. There will be times when I'm going to let go of certain things, and times where he has to let go too.

Like many women of my generation, I grew up with a notion that everything in a relationship was supposed to be "equal." If it felt that I was putting effort into something that Alec wasn't, it would really bother me. I did my best to meet him halfway on everything and get together with him during his windows of free time. I wanted him to be a part of my activities, too, and I had a big wake-up call when I entered the pregnancy and childbirth era of my life. My idea of partnership was completely upended.

When I was first pregnant with our oldest daughter,

Carmen, Alec and I had been together for nearly two years. I attempted to get Alec to come to every single ob-gyn appointment, scan, and blood test. But it just wasn't something he was comfortable with. We would bicker and fight and be late to appointments, and eventually it became more about us fighting and less about the excitement of having a baby.

I went into labor with Carmen at 3:30 a.m. I walked around our bedroom for hours, breathing through the contractions. Alec was in bed. Every once in a while he'd ask me if I was all right. (He has learned that when I'm in pain, I like my space. Maybe it's my independent nature?) Finally, after a few hours, when my contractions grew closer together, I knew it was time to go to the hospital. Alec said okay; he just had to walk the dogs first. While this sounds ridiculous or like those memes of fathers who are shit during labor, I've learned over the years that this type of rigid ritual is part of his OCD. And any annoyance I feel about it is only magnified within him. He didn't want to walk the dogs, but he didn't know how to function any other way. He was so overwhelmed by my being in labor that his rituals went into overdrive in a desperate attempt to calm himself.

The more I learned about OCD, the less judgmental and angry I became when he'd act this way. It doesn't mean that it's an excuse, just an explanation and a solid jumping-off point to work on our problems. A place of knowledge and understanding, not shame and anger and labeling as a bad person.

As I held on to the doorman's desk in between contractions, waiting for our ride, Alec would call from the street, ridiculously giving me updates on which of our dogs had pooped and peed. It bothered me on every possible level. (The doorman, a father himself, was probably praying that I didn't give birth right there in the lobby.)

Alec finally finished with the dogs and accompanied me to the hospital. The rest of the labor, Alec wasn't quite sure what to do or say. But when it finally did come time to push, he was right there—present and focused and truly with me, completing this miraculous thing we had done together by cutting our baby daughter's umbilical cord. While I'm not good at accepting help, I was grateful to have Alec's in that moment. It was incredible. Eventually, we got to hold Carmen and be together as a little family. It was like going down the wildest waterslide ever. I immediately looked at Alec and said, "I want to do that again!"

But when I got pregnant a year and change later with our son Rafa, Alec and I were no longer newlyweds, and this time around we had even less patience for each other. We fought a lot. Alec was traveling for work, and I would be alone at night in our apartment, pregnant with Rafa, Carmen in bed with me so I could nurse her. Once, very early in the morning, the dogs woke me up, wanting to go out. I put Carmen in the baby carrier over my pregnant belly, took a leash in each hand, and walked the dogs through a blanket of snow that had covered the city streets overnight. I was careful to avoid places where the dogs could get salt on their paws. (We'd been struggling with getting the dogs to wear their booties, so instead I put a special balm on their paws to give them protection against the salt.)

As I awkwardly walked in the thicker snow, I bent down,

trying to balance my stomach and Carmen and keep hold of the dogs as I picked up their poop. It was quite a physical feat. And just at that moment, a man drove by and screamed that I was a monster because my dogs didn't have boots on. That was it. I'd had enough and I broke. Achy, tired, defeated, and alone, I started to cry. Piece of shit. How dare you? Afterward, I knew it was silly to have gotten so emotional over a random guy yelling at me, but I was overwhelmed, and it was the last thing I needed to hear.

At this point, Alec had joined a play that would run in the Hamptons through June, and I was due to give birth to Rafa in July. Throughout the pregnancy, I had a feeling that he was going to be born early, but everyone brushed it off, saying it was my anxiety. But I was right: I went into labor at 2:30 a.m. on June 16, just shy of thirty-six weeks.

A few hours later, I saw my doctor in his office, and he gave me tricks to try to slow the labor down. It was too early to have Rafa, and we wanted to see if I could calm the contractions. So I returned home and went to bed, trying to rest on my sides. Occasionally, Alec would nervously enter our bedroom and ask me if I was having the baby or not so he could update work on when he would be returning. I sent him running out of the room each time with expletive-filled rants as an answer to his stupid questions. Eventually we realized that the labor was still progressing, not slowing down, and I had to go back to the doctor around 5:00 p.m.

Our driver took us; Alec's assistant was with us too. As we were driving uptown in the rush-hour traffic, with all those bumps and stops, I moaned and breathed through the pain. Alec was taking calls and responding to emails. Now I know that it was his way of dealing with stress, but at the time it really pissed me off, and I didn't hesitate to tell him so. Our driver and assistant spoke up: "Alec, this needs to wait." It is fascinating watching people wired like him: they can have hearts of gold, but stressful situations bring out behaviors that can misrepresent them.

Rafa was born at 1:21 a.m. on June 17. He came out with the umbilical cord wrapped around his neck multiple times. My doctor put him on my chest but he was blue and gasping. Quickly realizing this, they whisked him away to work on him. He was in an alcove adjacent to where I was, in the bed I had delivered him in. Nearly everyone was huddling around him and I couldn't see what was happening. I sat up and called out to them, begging to know how my son was. It felt like an eternity, and still no answer. I got more and more upset and said to a nurse, "If you don't wheel me over there, I am going to pull out my IVs and walk over there myself!" I have proudly told this story for years, and bless my friend who burst my bubble of feeling intimidating when he finally said to me, "Hilaria, you had an epidural, right?" "Of course," I responded. He countered with: "How were you going to pull your IVs out and march over there, demanding to see Rafa? Like, you couldn't feel your legs or walk . . ."

Rafa began breathing but needed to go to the NICU. Alec had to return to work because of his role in the play in the Hamptons. And so I had to take care of our NICU baby in the hospital and our toddler at home. Three days later, I brought

Rafa home in an Uber and fumed that my husband wasn't by my side while also knowing that contractually he had no choice. It felt like I was being disrespected because he wasn't there with me. And this poked at my ego.

That year was probably the rockiest for us, and not just in terms of juggling a baby and a toddler. I was so focused on how I thought things should be, and Alec was so set in his ways. Neither one of us would budge. I took my rings off as a sign that I was potentially ready to walk. Entering into a relationship as cement blocks will end in divorce, and that was where we were heading. We had to warm up and melt our solid selves, be willing to look within and see how we could do better. After doing much work on our relationship and getting to a better place, we eventually renewed our vows for our five-year anniversary.

Years later, I was at an influencer dinner, chatting with the woman sitting next to me. Alec and I had just celebrated ten years together, and I was talking about how we had renewed our vows at five. "Oh, people only renew their vows when their marriage is in trouble," she said snidely. She looked at me and I blinked at her. "Yup, tracks right," I said. Then I turned to have a conversation with someone else.

I got pregnant with Leo when Rafa was six months old. I think this both added to the stressful time in our marriage and, in some ways, forced us to save it. My frustration with

Alec during the first two pregnancies led to some independence with the third. I realized I didn't need Alec to accompany me through every experience in my life in order to feel equal; I questioned why I'd felt that way in the first place. I didn't need him to come with me to every doctor's appointment, and I didn't need to control the way he experienced stress relating to the pregnancies and labor and birth. With Leo, I went to more appointments alone—Alec did come to some—and I had more fun. Alec wanted to know what was happening at all the appointments and to see the ultrasounds he missed, but sometimes it was better for his anxiety, therefore my happiness, for me to go alone. Sitting in the doctor's office, waiting for the ob-gyns and techs to say that everything is okay, is always nerve-racking. I get it. I found that, by letting go, I took a step into my power. It was liberating. Now I always try to think of how I can steer my life toward happiness rather than make myself miserable by agonizing over what I should and shouldn't do.

Every pregnancy is different.

My pregnancy with Leo was pretty uneventful, but at the end of it I was low on amniotic fluid. I went for a scan to check on the water levels, and the doctor told me to head to the hospital to have the baby. I was having a lot of contractions, as I was close to my due date, but I wasn't in full labor yet.

It was a warm, late summer day and I took my time getting there. I decided that I wouldn't tell Alec I was going to have the baby until I got organized and settled and definitely had my epidural! At the hospital, I remember calmly putting the flip-flops that I was wearing in a closet and hanging up my dress, then changing into the hospital gown. I got connected to the monitors, and a friend came in to be with me. It was so different from my two previous pregnancies. "You're in labor," the nurse told me. "Good thing you came in."

I called our assistant, as well as friends and family, and swore them to secrecy about my whereabouts and labor. "After the last time, I cannot handle Alec until I get my epidural," I half-jokingly said. Once I was all hooked up and in less pain, I called him and told him where I was, that I'd been hanging out with one of my best friends and was feeling proud of myself for the way I had managed the experience.

I think he was half relieved and half annoyed. He rushed up to the hospital and we had a couple of hours before it was time to push. Leo came out after five minutes of pushing, and the nurse put him on my chest. He was pink and screaming his head off. It was my first skin-to-skin contact with one of my children when my baby hadn't been whisked away from me, which was incredible. I kept asking them when they were going to take him, and the nurse laughed at me and said, "He's yours! You get to keep him!"

It was during this pregnancy with Leo that I was able to find and appreciate my independence. I wasn't keeping track of what Alec was doing versus what I was doing. We weren't keeping score. We were just living our lives side by side, appreciating our strengths, acknowledging our weaknesses, meeting at a point of partnership. I was able to embrace the good in Alec, knowing that he cares. That his interpretation of love and partnership doesn't look like my former millennial expectations, and I am happier for having evolved.

If you'd told me before I had kids that this would happen, I might have judged myself as a woman who was weak and afraid to fight for equality with her husband—but I have learned that

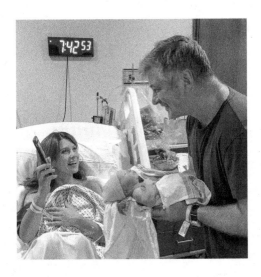

this has nothing to do with equality, and I have learned to have the courage to allow Alec to be Alec and me to be me. And, in return, I've felt a tremendous sense of peace and recognized my value and strength.

It was December of 2020, the middle of Covid, before vaccines had come out, and I'd just had my fifth child, Edu. Marilu was expected, via surrogate, in February. I'd just broken my ankle, and I was in a therapeutic boot. We took quarantine very seriously: I was terrified, as I had a newborn, and I was scared for Alec, who had to work on the set of the TV series *Dr. Death*, where he would be in close proximity with dozens of people.

I tried to lean into gratitude for how lucky we were and positivity from my children around me. But we all remember what it was like back then. It was just hard. It was the holidays, and I couldn't see my family because they were in a different country. I'd just had a baby but I had broken my ankle while running. I was trying my best to homeschool in a system where schools and teachers and parents and kids were all struggling. And then suddenly people were poking at me for how I sounded and how I code switched. It all got out of control. There was a coordinated mob after me at a time when people were at home, lonely, angry, and bored. Cancellation became the new gladiator sport. Especially against women. I have a strong feeling that one day our kids or kids' kids will be learning about the level of evil toxicity spewed at one another during this time.

Labels such as multicultural, multilingual, third-culture kids, culturally fluid, are attempts to capture what it is to belong and not to belong in a world that just wants to put everyone in one simple box. We often gravitate toward one another. We sound different because we naturally code switch between different languages and mannerisms. I had a crash course in how some monolingual people really struggle with how I speak. Switching is normal for me because I'm constantly going back and forth between two languages. Separating the two completely is like doing yoga and being told you can't be flexible. It was miserable trying to explain it on the world stage. It just is what it is and I didn't know how to be any different. Explaining language and brain function to the world was the last thing I ever thought I would have to do, and, unsurprisingly, I was unprepared. Now I am, because you bet super-literal and nerdy me has done as much research as I can get my hands on about how the brain develops and communicates through language! I try to laugh about it now, but it sure broke me. I am happy to see that what I went through back then is now being normalized. Online algorithms have flooded my feeds with memes of the flops of millions and the forgetfulness, but also how cool it is to speak multiple languages. I realize that I'm far from being alone. My friend Besher Jabri, who is in medical school and studied language and brain function, shared with his Instagram followers his thoughts when someone questions bilingualism:

"If you know how to speak more than one language, you need to know how your brain switches from language A to language B. For your brain to understand languages that are spoken to you, it activates Wernicke's area, and to produce language, it activates Broca's area. But let's say you're talking in one language, and then there's that one phrase in the other language that you just can't translate properly, so you need to switch languages. Then, this activates your prefrontal cortex. Now, to make this transition as smooth as possible, we need help from the anterior cingulate cortex, which will basically just make sure that there are no conflicts between language A and language B, and this can be like using grammar of one language in the other language or still sticking to one language. And it'll also signal to inhibit one language.

"Now, when the anterior cingular cortex signals to inhibit the first language, it actually goes to the basal ganglia, and this will actually suppress language A and make sure you're only speaking in language B. And another fun conflict that can arise is when switching languages to language B, you can still say a word in language A, but you just use the accent in language B, and this happens to me all the time."

Yes, this is all super complex, as is the brain around the use of multiple languages.

Another factor that made me very uncomfortable at the time is that I have ADHD and dyslexia, and these greatly impact my speech, my reading, my listening, my focus, my memory, and my self-confidence. This explains why I am super active. If we can have a light moment after so much darkness for me: I have a brain that is one part English, one part Spanish, seven dollops of mom brain, a heavy pour of distraction when I get stuck or go off on tangents and forget what I am saying while I am saying it . . . If you only knew how loud it is in my brain at any given moment! At that point, I had not discussed any of this publicly. I just existed in a land where sometimes I spoke one language and sometimes I spoke another, sometimes I mixed them and got mixed up, and I never talked about my processing differences. I just tried to be "normal."

Growing up being neurodivergent, I had to work harder in school than many of the people around me. I never felt like I was smart in the right way. I am relieved that now there's less of a stigma around differences in learning and processing. This has given me the freedom to shed some of the shame I felt for so long. I'm now aware that my brain just works differently and I can really succeed in the right environments and tasks. It's something I've struggled with my entire life, and even though I tried to ignore it, I marvel at how I settled into certain environments where I thrived, like New York City and teaching yoga. I knew I had to stay active in order to function and think clearly.

Now I know that it's ridiculous that anyone would feel outraged or amused because someone forgot a word. Can you be honest right now, reading this: Have you ever forgotten a word? But back then, I started to really unravel. I was confused. I felt lost. I missed my family. I couldn't eat. I got very thin. I started to question my sanity. I started to question if I was a good person. I returned to what I used to do as a child, and started to call myself stupid. When I woke up, I wanted to be dead. And I got worse and worse and worse.

I'd sit on my bathroom floor, nursing my baby Edu at 3:00 a.m., and speak to my brother in Spain, and I'd cry to him, nauseous about it all. He'd try to lighten things up by saying, "Can we just stop for a second and talk about how nonsensical this is? You're speaking to me in Spain, where I've lived for most of my life, in Spanish, about the validity of our connection to Spain. No one is really offended—it's Covid, and they are home alone and bored, and there is so much misinformation." I teach my kids Spanish, we eat certain Spanish foods that I grew up eating, and these are comforts to me. My brother raised his son in Spain, obviously immersed in Spanish culture and language, and made sure that my nephew spoke English and learned American culture too. Being this way is not taking anything from anyone. It's just the way that we were raised.

I read an amazing article in the sports section of the *New York Times* about pro soccer players and how, when they switch teams to a different country, it's normal that their accents and voices and speech change and—wait for it—they forget words! Not only did this very insightful article say it's normal and expected, but it also pointed out that it shows empathy in communication and is a good thing. I love to see these topics spoken about more and more because it's just true and it hits close to home. I am not a male soccer player, though, and, looking back, I have learned that it isn't just malice and ignorance that led to the insanity I experienced; it really was about a woman and her voice. Taking her voice.

*

Alec was so good to me throughout this time. He had experienced similar situations: people saying awful things about him, trying to destroy him, making others think he was a bad person. He could reach out from a place of real empathy and personal experience. In the middle of the night, I'd wake up and remember what was happening to me. And he was always there. He'd know I was awake, and he would hold me close and say, "You're not alone. I'm here and I love you. And you can cry, because I know how much it hurts. It's so awful, but just know what they're saying is not true." Then he would make me laugh: "And even if it were true, it would be stupid and inoffensive. What are you? A spy? You created a fake identity? You immediately learned a new language? To make me fall in love with you? I mean, that is a big effort," he joked. "Am I worth it? Take it as a compliment: whatever they are saying you did would make you a genius, and we should use you as a government agent to protect the United States."

For years afterward, when I would hear a recording of my voice, I'd cringe because I hated the sound of it. I took speech therapy to enunciate better. The more I got treatment for the ADHD that I was trying to ignore, the better I got at separating the two languages and not getting as distracted. I tried to improve myself in all the ways the internet trolls had told me I was broken. And then I got to the point where I realized: *This is not helping me. I am mixed-up but I am not bad or broken.* And then Hilaria returned.

The same defiant Hilaria who refused to fill out a Valentine's Day card that was demanded of her; the Hilaria who chased

Alec out of our bedroom when he was saying things that were stressing her out when she was laboring with Rafa. The Hilaria who cleaned out the pantry. I don't have to change myself because of negative people misrepresenting me. I have spent too much time being my stubborn self to let them hurt me anymore.

I do sound different, depending on who I am talking to, how tired I am, how revved up I am about something. It just is what it is and it's not a bad thing—far from it. It's normal. I know who I am, I like who I am, and who I am makes sense based on how I was raised and how I live my life. I've learned that to be told to prove yourself to others just because you are different is a form of abuse. On an academic level, I am proud of all I have learned about the human brain and language and belonging. Back then, instead of standing up for myself, I hung my head and apologized. But now I have compassion for myself because I didn't know how to act any differently: it was all so confusing and unexpected. Now I choose not to be intimidated and not to feel like a victim. And I hope by speaking up and living this way, there can be better understanding of people who sound different. Shit was thrown at me, and it took me a while, after feeling wounded and broken, but I got back up again. With Alec by my side, I am determined to live as my multi-mix me.

*

While I believe Alec and I are equals, I realize we aren't the same. He thrives with tasks like bringing the kids to school every day and often picking them up. He goes to parent meetings at school and is great at organizing playdates. I don't do well in these situations, and so I've freed myself from much of this. I forget to call people back and get overwhelmed. Though I am always present for my children, I sometimes retreat from the outside world. I think some of this is remnant trauma from being picked apart publicly, some of it is just being a tired mom, and some of it is definitely my neurodiverse brain. I feel lucky that I have a partner who is very gregarious and wonderful at logistics. I shine privately with my children, so I do homework with them, play with them, bring them to their doctor's visits. I feed them and bathe them and put them to bed. Each baby has slept in between the two of us as I nursed them for at least a year. We are always playing and dancing in the house and spending so much time together.

Through years of getting it wrong and right, Alec and I have gotten to a place of being able to see each other and accept help

from each other. When one of us is struggling, the other says, "I've got this." It is a process of letting go of beliefs that keep us stuck so that we can evolve. I have to say that Alec has been better at letting go than I am. He knows himself, perhaps because of his age and experience. I had to learn through my twenties and thirties about myself and my strengths, and one of the most important and daunting tasks was admitting when I needed help.

Alec sent me a tabloid article recently, another prediction that our marriage was in trouble. We try to find humor in these kinds of things. This article was a jab at how hard these past few years have been for us, with all Alec has been through. But it was also a jab at me because it alleged that Alec was having financial problems and was afraid I would leave him. At this point, after all the many articles that have been written about our family, does this make me mad? Sure. Does it keep me up at night? No. But I feel like we should all be beyond this in our culture.

After all the learning and growing we've experienced as a couple, Alec and I are in the best place we've ever been. The future is unknown, but right here and now we are a good team. We love each other and our children. We have had our ups and downs, but we chose to work on making it work. Alec and I have been lucky enough to be compatible despite our natures being completely opposite. Who knows what will come? Nothing is a forever guarantee, but now, every day, we laugh. We also drive each other crazy, but that's part of the joy of life.

2

MOM BOSS

While we may come to motherhood in different ways—adoption, surrogacy, giving birth, stepparenting, guardianship—whatever route we take, we are united by our desire to give all the love we have to another being. It's an animal instinct that some of us have: an excess of love that we need to pour into someone else. The giving of this love is the most fulfilling gift I have ever experienced. I have also learned that when this love is unfulfilled due to infertility or broken as a result of loss, it is so painful. It can hurt so much to be a mother who no longer has a place to put all that extra love. There is no hierarchy with the label "mother," for all motherly love is equal, regardless of the path.

As mothers, we are built to go above and beyond and, as a result, we are able to do incredible things. I don't just mean those stories of super strength—mothers helping their kids in emergencies—but the more common experiences of motherhood. Staying up all night with a teething baby, dealing with a teenager who is struggling, exercising the patience needed to get through difficult phases, and having that intuition that tells us when something's not quite right.

As women, motherhood bonds us in so many ways, but I've also found that it can be an extremely competitive and judgmental space. This is a pain that we probably all know too well and is one of the themes I would like to tackle in this chapter. Can we open up the parameters of "mother" and allow people to use the term without judgment? We all just want to do what is best for our kids: It's hard enough as is, so why do we need to make it harder on each other? Have I judged? Yes. Have I misunderstood people? Yes. Have I been judged and misunderstood by others? One hundred percent yes.

Breast or bottle? Homemade or store-bought? Organic or not? Co-sleep or sleep train? Put the hat on or take the hat off? What I've learned from having children is that there are a million different ways to mother. I don't want to make things harder for my fellow moms by opening my mouth to preach about how things "should" be done. I do my best now to resist being judgmental, gossipy, and competitive.

When I feel jealousy, I notice it and try to turn it into admiration rather than envy. I check myself and know that those feelings, while common, are weaknesses. I ask the question: *What's making me judge another mom? Why do I feel my way is better?* I try to give every mom the benefit of the doubt. *Will my judgment improve a situation?* (Said by literally not one person, ever.) Can I learn from a different way someone is mothering? What would it cost me to just let someone else be as they are, as they choose? We never know what someone else is going through. There's no magic button to press to achieve this. It takes practice and awareness.

Breast versus bottle? I've had experience with both. With Carmen, I didn't start pumping until she was about a week old. I hadn't really done any research about breastfeeding and I didn't have a clear idea of how I wanted to do things. I ended up co-sleeping, although I'd never expected to do that. And it was because I was breastfeeding. I'd put her down, get into my bed, and then she'd start screaming again, so I'd pick her up and bring her to our bed. Alec and I are both very stationary, very light sleepers, so co-sleeping was safe for us, though I know it's a very controversial thing. I co-slept with all my babies, and so you can imagine that sometimes there were a lot of people in our bed!

I only pumped a little bit now and then, because I don't like pumping. It's a boring activity and it seems to take forever. But I did want to have some milk stored, because I wanted to be able to go out occasionally. I breastfed Carmen for about fifteen months and then ended up weaning her pretty abruptly because I became pregnant with Rafa. I was told that breast-feeding while pregnant can be dangerous because when you have that letdown of milk, it creates contractions of the uterus. I felt awful weaning Carmen that way. I have learned through breastfeeding my babies that I prefer it when the baby self-weans. I now know that tandem nursing can be totally safe, but I was scared back then.

With Rafa, I started pumping earlier, right after he was born. He was in the NICU at first, with just a few complications. He was fine, but we were nervous those first few days. The doctors wanted to make sure he was getting enough milk, so they started to talk about formula, but I was very focused on breastfeeding. I pumped more because of that.

I got pregnant with Leo when Rafa was six months old, and one of the ways I knew I was pregnant was that my milk production crashed. I went to the doctor and said, "I'm pregnant." He said, "You're not pregnant." But I could tell I was because of the change in my milk. A week later, the pregnancy test came back positive.

I continued to breastfeed Rafa. I wasn't afraid that I was going to lose the baby because of breastfeeding; I'd done more research and I knew my body better. But my milk eventually dried up by the time Rafa was ten months old. And I had very little milk stored up—like, hardly anything. So then I had to move on to . . . *the dreaded formula!* I'm joking: it was totally fine. It made me realize the whole breast-versus-bottle thing is such a ridiculous source of stress that women put on themselves and each other. I continued to breastfeed my other babies, but I have no problem with formula. I feel a little like, *Oh, stop it, everybody!* That was a big learning experience for me. Why is there so much shaming? The shaming is real.

When Leo was born, I started pumping right away. Even though we had a great experience with formula, I wanted to breastfeed and store my own milk. They had the pumps in the hospital, and I used those and brought milk home, and that's when I figured out this trick:

In the beginning, I pump every hour that I am awake for just three minutes. I do it even if nothing comes out, and then I put the pump away. I didn't have the energy to wash it every time, so I'd just put it back in the fridge with drops of milk on it. Eventually this method taught my body to make milk faster, because, often, the more a baby nurses (or the more you pump), the more milk comes. (This is how it works feeding twins, triplets, and so forth.) Obviously, every body is different and breastfeeding isn't for all. See above: formula feeds just fine too. (Insert millennial wink emoji here.)

I tricked my body into thinking that I had more than one baby drinking milk. And lo and behold, it worked! I also knew I had to be extremely hydrated. At first, I drank only coconut water. Then I moved on to energy drinks—but only the natural ones. Then, eventually, I moved on to plain old Gatorade. Younger me would have totally judged me for that, but it worked really well, and I am over being intimidated by unsolicited opinions, mine or others; that's so early 2020s. With this method, I could pump for three minutes and would get a full bottle, whereas with my earlier babies, I'd pump for thirty minutes and get an ounce or so because I wasn't doing it as frequently or staying as hydrated. I prefer to do it more frequently for less time. Usually, I could get the milk going pretty quickly, but if I ever had a problem, I would just put the baby to my breast for like thirty seconds. It is wild to see how no matter what machines we humans invent, the body reacts differently to the baby versus the machine. The fact that my baby could get my body to give milk and the body was refusing to give it to the pump sometimes was incredible. The milk would come, I'd put the baby in my lap, and then I'd pump for three minutes. Even if the baby was fussy and angry, I eventually learned to not feel bad about it: I was making a bottle for them! A wise older mother told me no baby ever died from just crying. Good advice: straight to the point. It seemed harsh and strange when I first heard it, but eventually I found it soothed me during a baby's screaming moments. It allowed me to relax, think more clearly, and be a better and calmer mother.

When we'd go on trips or do day activities, I'd make a little kit for myself. I'd put my pump in a backpack and take inside and outside adapters with me. I know where every single outlet is in the Brooklyn Botanic Garden. I'd have the milk bags and bring ziplock bags and a little cooler to store them in. Walking around with the pump just gave me more freedom. You don't have that much freedom when you're pumping, and I wanted to be a good and present mom for my older children too.

It was all just a part of my motherhood journey. I ate more during that time: lots of nutrient-rich foods. You're so hungry when you're breastfeeding and pumping! With the last four babies, I had four giant freezers entirely filled with milk. People would ask me, "What are you going to do with all that milk?" And I'd say, "They will drink it! They will drink it because I made it!" And, for the most part, they have.

※

When we first started dating, Alec let me know right away that he had a teenage daughter.

At that time, I basically lived under a rock—or on a yoga mat—and he soon learned that he had to tell me things about himself that many others knew already or would just google.

My only real points of reference to stepparenting were the evil stepmothers in Disney movies and fairy tales. I had no idea what to expect. But I did know that I had tremendous respect for family and didn't want to cause any harm. So, before I met his daughter Ireland for the first time, I told Alec that if she didn't like me or didn't feel comfortable with me, I would go my own way and not continue seeing him. He gets so mad at me when I remind him of this now, as it still brings up feelings that I was going to abandon him. But I believed that it would have been the right thing to do. I would never want to cause her or their relationship any stress or difficulty.

Fortunately, Ireland was so welcoming and kind to me from the first moment we met. We have had the best relationship over the years, based on mutual respect. There were a few factors that were working in our favor. Firstly, it had been quite a while since Alec and his ex-wife, Kim, had split. Both had had relationships since, with people whom Ireland had met and knew (and sometimes tortured . . . and would wickedly tell me about with the best sense of humor: total *Parent Trap* vibes).

I also think it helped that I came in with the understanding that a family existed already. Alec wasn't just my boyfriend: he was a father and, very importantly, his daughter had a mother who deserved my respect.

When invited into their family, I always made myself available. I never pushed and never asserted myself. I love Ireland and she loves me, and I was able to be another outlet for her when she needed support or to check in about something. I am eleven years older than Ireland—when we met, I was twenty-seven and she was nearly sixteen—which puts me right in the middle between her age and Alec and Kim's ages.

Ireland becoming a sister when she was nearly eighteen is a story that one day she may tell. But I know that my children love their big sister and love being *tios/tias* to Ireland's daughter, Holland. We all feel very lucky to be part of our wild and blended family.

Growing up, I didn't think much about marriage or kids. I assumed that my desire to be a mother would eventually kick in, but it wasn't something I was focused on when I met Alec.

Alec, however, was very clear that he wanted to have more

children, and so I started to think about it seriously. We got married and, five months later, I found out I was pregnant. Excited and terrified, I immediately went to our local bookstore and bought *What to Expect When You're Expecting*. I asked for it to be giftwrapped, pretending it was for someone else while attempting to keep my pregnancy a secret. (The salesperson told me years later that she'd known, and we had a good laugh about how I thought I was being super-stealthy.) I didn't actually finish reading the book, because it was filled with worst-case scenarios. The more I read about pregnancy, the more my twenty-eight-year-old self discovered that it is really scary and lots of bad things can happen! So I decided to drop the research, figuring it was a situation that was probably going to go in only one direction. When you get to know me, this is quintessential Hilaria. Welp! Let's go with the flow! I trusted my doctor and just went through it month by month, a bit like an ostrich burying its head in the sand.

That said, I was a very vigilant ostrich! Every cramp would scare me, and I would race to the bathroom, sure I was bleeding. I hate oatmeal but heard that it was good for a baby's brain development, so I tried to eat it. It made me vomit, so I didn't stay the course on that one. I did manage to skip drinking coffee, and remained active (but not too active), and was mindful about what I ate, avoiding things that my doctor had recommended pregnant women stay away from.

When I was around nineteen weeks pregnant, I went to visit my family in Spain. After I flew back to New York, the next day I developed horrible cramps. I was having dinner with a friend, and every few minutes I would be in pain. He said, "I think you're having contractions and need to call your doctor." Alarmed, I did, and my doctor told me I was dehydrated from the plane ride and needed to drink Gatorade. I stupidly blurted out, "I am so sorry, but I don't drink things that color." He basically told me to get my butt to the bodega and pick some up. I drank it, it worked, and the pains subsided.

Closer to my due date, I began to genuinely wonder: How does one get a baby out? I hadn't taken any birthing classes; I'd been too anxious to even read about it! To give myself comfort, I'd look around at every person I saw and would think: *You were a baby, and you, and you. This must be possible, and I will find out when the time comes!* These people around me had come out! It helped me remember that people have been having babies forever, and that I could do this. This might seem silly, but sometimes I function with childlike simplicity.

I didn't know much about labor when I had my first child other than I was supposed to head to the hospital when my contractions were five minutes apart, lasted for sixty seconds, and "hurt like hell," according to my ob-gyn. Three days before Carmen's due date, at 3:30 a.m., I went into labor. I walked, I counted, I stretched for hours. At around 7:00 a.m., I called my mother and told her what was happening. She asked if I'd called my doctor, and I told her I hadn't because I didn't want to bother him in the middle of the night. (I'm constantly working on my issues with feeling bad about asking for help when I need it.) I finally called him, and he gave me an earful about how it was his job to get calls from women in labor any time of day or night and I shouldn't feel like I was bothering him.

Carmen's birth was the wildest ride I'd ever been on. I couldn't believe that I'd pushed her out, that she was here, that she had ten fingers and toes and a face and was a whole person. It was absolutely mind-blowing to me. I loved her immediately, and as the first night went on, it started to sink in that I'd made it through the part that I'd been terrified of. But . . . now what? How do I mother? Suddenly, pushing a seven-pound person out seemed like an easy feat compared to keeping a tiny human safe. The panic that I began to feel was overwhelming. In the hospital, I had to watch videos about shaken baby syndrome and keeping your child safe from abduction. My anxiety spiked, and I decided the only reasonable solution was to watch her all the time and never sleep again. Unsurprisingly, that wasn't a sustainable tactic.

While I was pretty insecure as a first-time mom, little by little we found our way, Carmen and me. I started to realize that my baby was going to wake up, my baby was going to sleep, my baby was going to eat. I was going to be able to do this.

Through having babies, I have learned that society often connects motherhood to physical pain and suffering in a very specific way. While I have had six babies in a more traditional way, I have learned through my losses, my baby born via surrogate, and having a stepdaughter that paths may look different, but when our babies are here, we love them just the same. We have as strong a bond with each, and we are all very much worthy of the title "mother."

RouShoots

✳

One thing I've learned is that if we're going to open ourselves up to the joy of the good things in life, we're also going to experience pain. We're going to get hurt. It's a fact of life. Pain and joy are two sides of the same coin, and I often think that we only know one because we know the other.

When pregnancy loss comes up in conversation, and I share that I've experienced it, oftentimes other mothers open up to me, and we can support each other. It's a horrible club to belong to, yet one that's often a part of childbearing. I am happy that in my lifetime we've become more open about it, paving the way for others to do the same. I don't know if it's something we ever truly heal from. I know my losses will always be a sad page in the book of my life and have forever changed me and the way I mother.

I've had a few chemical pregnancies over the years, mostly between my pregnancies with Carmen, Rafa, Leo, and Romeo, from the ages of twenty-nine to thirty-four. I found out I was pregnant again in the spring, but, from the beginning, the baby never had a strong heartbeat. Some of the doctors I spoke to said, "Well, you're thirty-five now"—which is to say I was old in their book—"and let's remember that one in five pregnancies ends in loss . . . you have four children, this is number five, and you are the perfect statistic. When you were younger, you had smoother pregnancies; now that you are 'geriatric' or have AMA—advanced maternal age—this is what happens." I found this hard to accept. I had had Romeo the year before and everyone was telling me how young I was at thirty-four! It seemed ridiculous that just a year later I was considered "geriatric." That is the fascinating thing about being a woman: first we are too young to be taken seriously; then, in the blink of a birthday, we are past our "prime."

For me, thirty-five was also the age at which I was no longer willing to put up with all the secrecy and shenanigans of keeping my life hidden from the public. There was a market for information about me, often fabricated and untrue, and so the way I decided to deal with it was to get ahead of it by sharing my own news first. At the time, I felt like this was a win and a way to take hold of my power; now I think it was a trauma response to having my boundaries violated so many times, for so many years. I don't fault myself, but I have learned to have the courage and confidence not to give myself away as I once did.

In the past, I'd had upsetting experiences with my pregnancy "reveals." When I was pregnant with Carmen and just nearing twelve weeks, I went to New Orleans for the Super Bowl. (Alec was hosting the NFL Honors.) I was nauseous and tired, and a supposed friend told me I should go and get some sun—that vitamin D had helped his wife when she was pregnant. So I put on a bathing suit and lay by the pool. Little did I know, the person I considered a confidant had set me and my little baby bump up to be photographed, outing me and sharing my pregnancy news with the world before I had even let friends know. When I found out a day later, there were articles that included speculations on my weight gain, the stage of my pregnancy . . . Plus I was hurt that someone I knew well would betray my trust so maliciously. This was my news to share, and it felt like something had been taken from me—a feeling that would become all too familiar in the years to come. I constantly hear, "You signed up for this"; "You asked for this"; "It comes with the territory"; and my favorite: "You're probably used to it." But let me tell you this: you never get used to that kind of violation.

Years later, knowing I was losing my pregnancy, I decided to question why we didn't talk about miscarriages while they were happening. Dealing with so much sadness and pain—physical and emotional—from a loss like this and not being able to reach out to others to tell them what you are going through felt like a ridiculous societal norm.

I decided to talk about this issue on the *Today* show before any other news outlet got the story. I hoped it would help other women experiencing the same thing and potentially open up space for those who might want to talk about their own losses. I discussed why we are expected to pretend to be strong and okay, when we are suffering.

I was terrified about bringing up this subject, but I am glad that I did. It felt good to share and connect with a community of women, many of whom wrote messages to me about their own miscarriage experiences. Some women shared that every year they secretly celebrated the due date of the pregnancy they lost as their child's birthday. They were living with the identity crisis of feeling like a mother but not being able to check that societal box. These women are mothers to me, and our shared pain and experience helps me to hold space for them in my heart.

After I left the *Today* show studio, I went directly to my ultrasound. My baby's heartbeat had fully stopped. I cried for myself and for this baby, even though I'd known it was inevitable.

❋

Soon after this miscarriage, once my HCG numbers hit "not pregnant," I decided to do in vitro fertilization for the first time. I was older, right? Or so some doctors kept telling me.

Someone said to me once, "I knew we were done having kids when I looked around at my children and knew that everyone was here who was supposed to be here." Alec and I weren't there yet and we did not yet feel complete as a family.

The IVF process is tough, as anyone who has gone through it knows. I have tremendous admiration for those who brave it. It's a journey. The constant blood draws, the injections, the patches, the suppositories, the mood swings, the swelling . . . the procedures.

I transferred an embryo and got pregnant, and I wanted to let people know about my pregnancy before the twelve-week mark. I think this was partly a desire to push at societal boundaries and partly from the unresolved trauma of my other pregnancy announcements being hijacked by the media. If I revealed it first, it would be mine to share. It was about ownership, autonomy, and agency, as so many things in my life now are.

And so I told the world. We knew it was a girl. I told Carmen that she was going to have a little sister. She was so excited. The three boys were too little to really understand. I stopped the hormones just shy of twelve weeks.

Starting with my pregnancy with Rafa, I began to feel the babies move during the first trimester. I didn't feel Carmen until nineteen weeks. Some say it feels like a flutter . . . It always felt more like a fish to me—something swimming around and grazing parts of my belly that I could pick up on as movement. I kept telling my doctors that it was weird that I didn't feel this baby move. They told me that it's uncommon to feel it so early and that everything was progressing really well. In so many ways, however, my IVF pregnancy felt different compared to my first four pregnancies. I felt off.

I went in for a scan between months four and five. I walked a lot, and I remember walking to my appointment and not feeling her moving. I tried not to worry, knowing I sometimes confuse anxiety with intuition, and that, according to the doctors, everything was fine. When I lay back on the exam table, Doina, an amazing technician who has taken care of me with all my babies, put the warm gel on my growing belly and then started with the probe. Then she paused. I looked at her and knew that what I'd been feeling was my intuition and not my anxiety. In a small, trembling voice I asked, "Is everything okay?"

"No, it isn't," she responded.

"Is she dead?" I asked.

"Yes."

I looked at the screen and saw the lifeless baby just floating there. I began to sob. When this happens, there is no way to make it better. It's simply horrible. I was escorted in to talk with the ultrasound doctor, whom I barely knew.

He sat me down and rolled through all the typical comments.

"This wasn't your fault. I know this is awful, but you are thirty-five now, and this is just bad luck—two in a row. But you have so many beautiful and healthy kids, and some women don't even have that."

I thanked him and left. And I walked, and I walked, and I walked.

I knew I had to tell Carmen; she was constantly asking about her little sister. Alec was on a Hampton Jitney bus coming back from Long Island. I called him first. I would have preferred to tell him in person but I couldn't keep it in. He cried. He was sitting just behind the bus driver and you aren't supposed to talk on your cell phone on board. The bus driver could tell something awful had happened and said to Alec: "You take all the time you need to talk to your wife."

As soon as I got home, I told Carmen. "I know I told you that your little sister was coming, but I was wrong, and she will come another time." I didn't know what else to say. I recorded our conversation on video, because I wanted to include Alec as well as I could in this process. I shared the video on my Instagram. I couldn't think of anything else to do. I just needed it to be out there; I couldn't handle any more congratulations. Not one. I thought it would break me. Maybe this sounds strange, but I also just needed it to be real, since it felt like a nightmare. My daughter hugged me and kissed me and was way more composed and wiser than I was. I learn so much from my children who are truly wise beyond their years.

My doctors helped me get a procedure booked for the next day, which I was relieved about because originally there was talk that it might be a few days before they could get my baby out. I don't know another way to put it: I slept with my dead child inside of me. I would wake up to realize it was true, cry, and then somehow doze off again. I would look down at my belly and couldn't believe something so connected with life was like a tomb. I remember thinking that I couldn't believe how many tears a body could produce. It was a weird desire to move past it while also fearing letting her go and no longer being with her. True grief.

That morning I set off for the hospital. Alec was meeting me there. I don't remember why we did it this way; perhaps he was with our older kids. My memory is so jumbled from this time. I was in an Uber, going uptown, and the driver was listening to the morning radio. The news came on, and at one point it said, "Some sad news: Alec and Hilaria Baldwin have had their second pregnancy loss in a row." It felt like my breath had been taken away. I leaned forward toward the driver and in a low, shaky voice said, "They are talking about me. This is me and I am going to have the baby taken out of me now and that is where you are driving me to."

He didn't respond.

"Sir? Sir?"

I was basically having an out-of-body experience. I thought

to myself, *What are you doing, Hilaria? Just stop talking and sharing!*

I leaned back, tearful, realized it was a blessing the man hadn't heard me, and soldiered on. At the doctor's, they wanted me to see my baby one more time before the procedure. I guess this was to help me really understand that she was gone. This makes so much sense, since finality is necessary when the mind is so tortured. Seeing her, floating lifeless again, was gut-wrenching.

This loss hit me hard. I'd gotten past all the scary milestones we worry about early on in pregnancy. Something bad still happened. My belly went down so fast, but my milk came in, because my body thought I had given birth. I'd never dried up milk before without nursing, and it was difficult. This is one of the reasons when people ask me if I have had seven children come out of me—a question I've heard more times than you can imagine—I never know what to say. This was the baby who was delivered and is not with us. My older children still ask me about their sister, and we talk about her as if she is one of them. And she *is* one of them because we keep her memory alive. Our time together was short, but she was here and I love her. We all do.

A few months later I found out I was naturally pregnant with Edu and I didn't know how to feel or how to tell anyone after the loss that had just happened. Covid hit, and because of the lockdown, I felt less pressure to tell everyone right away. I waited around five or six months to announce it. I had to get past the number of months at which I had lost the last baby. For my own peace of mind. April 30, 2020, had been her due date, and I think about that every time it comes. Like the women who'd shared their stories with me, I feel such a connection to this soul we lost.

✳

I have to admit that I first heard about surrogacy from salacious and offensive stories of celebrities needing to keep fit for a role and not wanting to gain weight and then have to lose it. It was about vanity and laziness. "Vending machine babies." I had heard that famous people didn't even raise their kids; nannies did. Celebrity children were accessories like handbags or small dogs. I hope this sounds ridiculous to you, because it is. I realize if I can be sold this bullshit, other people can too. I mean, how crazy is it that you can pay someone to have a baby for you—and they just give it to you? Or, as my ninety-plus-year-old grandfather asked me when I told him Marilu would be born via surrogacy: "Is it like a three-way baby?" He wasn't joking—and wasn't judging. He was the most open-hearted person in the world, and I loved him for his questions. He was simply trying to understand so that he could support us in the right way.

A side note about my grandfather: he was a veteran and straight, and he had one flag flying outside his home—the LGBTQIA+ flag. He wanted all to know that everyone was welcome and that "straight men didn't have to be so insecure about their own sexuality." Bless him.

During my pregnancy with Edu, my body felt like it did

with my earlier pregnancies—nothing like how it had reacted to the IVF pregnancy. I knew that I also wanted to use this other embryo I had. I was still hurting from our recent loss; I illogically blamed myself and I believed that my body had rejected IVF, and would do so again. I realize now how irrational this sounds, but back then that's how I felt.

We decided to explore surrogacy. I spoke with some of my friends who'd connected with surrogates for various reasons. One couple gave me the contact info of their surrogate. She now runs an agency specializing in surrogacy. When I spoke with her, she was so kind and incredibly informative. She told me about how much joy it gave her to help people have their children: "I help make families and love!" While this sounded noble and beautiful, I was worried about things that I now know are normal to question: Does it feel any less like your child if you don't give birth to it? Does the surrogate ever want to keep the baby? Is it cruel to take the baby from the surrogate? What kind of relationship do you have with someone who's doing something so incredible for you?

She patiently answered these questions and assured me that it was good to talk about all of this—that nothing I had asked was offensive. I have learned this in my own life. If anyone has the courage to ask me questions we normally feel we shouldn't, I smile and tell them that it's okay to ask. I asked the same questions. To ask from a place of genuinely wanting to learn, and then respecting the answer—that's the trick.

Since we were in the middle of Covid restrictions, I met potential surrogates on the phone. I clicked immediately with the woman who ended up carrying Marilu, and we are still very close. We see her whenever she's in New York, and she is an angel who is a part of our family forever.

She quickly explained to me how she viewed surrogacy: Imagine we are neighbors and I make a cake with my ingredients and my recipe. My oven doesn't work (or, in my case, with Edu, it was currently occupied). So I go to my neighbor's house and ask to use her oven to bake the cake. She says yes and gives my cake back to me when it's baked. My recipe, my ingredients, my cake. Her oven. This silly example made all the sense in the world.

Our surrogate has a young child herself, and she loved being pregnant. (She is one of those who say they feel "amazing" while pregnant. Well, that's a feeling I've never had!)

During my surrogate's pregnancy with Marilu, since we couldn't meet in person due to Covid, we spoke every day like two girlfriends going through all of it together, as I was pregnant with Edu and she with Lu. We would text and call with updates on kicks and hiccups, sleepless nights, and, yes, heartburn! We would FaceTime from our scans and send funny memes. Surrogacy was legalized in New York just before Marilu was born, and so we got to bring our amazing friend up to New York City to give birth here. Two historic women: Marilu and our surrogate, the first surrogate to give birth in New York and the first surrogate baby!

When she went into labor and was in the hospital, we FaceTimed with her family back home and went through everything together. Due to Covid policies, only one parent could be in the room, so Alec waited outside and I was there

throughout it all. I helped hold one of her legs and put the oxygen mask on her. I also gave her all the encouragement and the love that I'd been lucky enough to get from Alec during our five births. Marilu was born and it was amazing. I cut the cord, just like Alec had done with our other children, and then did skin-to-skin bonding with her.

Then I sat with our surrogate and Alec as we all just stared at this little person who'd been made from our three bodies. Our "three-way baby." We spent the night hanging out together in the hospital, celebrating and taking care of Marilu.

Telling the world was another task to tackle. Exhausted from all the opinions, I really didn't want to share my family and personal life at this point. I wanted to shut myself in and stay closed and private. But there were already rumors swirling, so I was advised to just announce it myself before someone else did and made the story something different from what it was.

I posted an overhead shot of Marilu on my lap with the other kids around me. The opinions came, and people's reactions ranged from extremely supportive to outright ignorant. To this day, I don't understand how anyone could be so cruel about another person's child and choices.

I am just as much Marilu's mother as I am to the other Baldwinitos. She belongs with us and she is one of us—her unique and special arrival is just a fun fact.

I see the story of Marilu's birth as not just standing on its own but also within the context of the baby I lost. All my children and their stories are connected and individual. Through my experience with surrogacy, I met such amazing people and learned so many important answers to the questions we aren't supposed to ask. I also realized that I had judged women too harshly when I had that idea in my mind of what surrogacy looked like—that women who used surrogates were just trying to convince the world that they were worthy of the title of "mom." How wrong I was.

I've endured cruel opinions, and have been deliberately misrepresented and the object of cheap jokes, but learning to rise above it all has given me the freedom to step into my own definition of being a mother. As always, the harshness never has anything to do with us anyway. And the definition of a mother is so much broader than I could ever have imagined. I know how it feels to be told we are doing it all wrong, and this is why I have evolved into being very open with my heart and protective of others who walk all sorts of paths. Just like my grandpa.

3

MANUAL NOT INCLUDED

Among the most common questions I get asked in interviews are: What is the best mom advice you have been given? And what is the best mom advice you can give? Because I've been asked these things so often over the past eleven-plus years of being a mother, I've attempted to perfect this single nugget of wisdom, but I don't think it's possible. There is no one right mother, one right child, one right family, or one right way. The most authentic thing I can do is tell mothers: You will get a lot of advice, some requested, some not. You can listen with the understanding that this is *their* experience of mothering. Ultimately, you are the mother in your home, the CEO making the decisions that you're comfortable with. Always be humble, always be willing to learn, and be flexible, but keep your feet firmly planted on the ground. You are just as worthy of being a mother as anyone else! You have as much right to be here in this community as the next mother.

I still have insecure moments where I think: *Am I getting this right? Am I screwing this whole thing up? Are my kids going to talk about this in therapy in twenty years? How do I be confident yet also admit when I am wrong? I want to mother with courage and humility.*

Up until the age of seven, Carmen didn't even know what a curse word was. But then came Rafa and Leo and Romeo, our boys, who curse left and right.

I tried ignoring it, then joking about it. Then I tried to get mad about it, but that didn't last, as we all just thought it was so funny to hear little kids being so naughty. The more kids you have, the earlier the little ones pick things up. Over the years, I've learned to let go of things I used to be controlling about. It's just part of being in a big family with so many kids so close in age.

We call Edu and Marilu the "Dedes." It is a term they came up with to refer to each other when they were babies babbling. While they aren't twins, they very much act like they are. They are inseparable and fiercely loyal and they finish each other's sentences. They also are very naughty together and started to swear when they were only one. My kids have always been early talkers, and I took some pride in this, but it also came with a downside when the words the older siblings were teaching were "fuck" and "bitch." Since we are a bilingual home, we decided to confuse the Dedes by telling them that "fuck" was the Spanish word *foca* (seal—the animal) and "bitch" and "beach" (*playa* in Spanish) are homophones, a term I learned from Carmen's second-grade English class. Little by little, when they would say the two bad words in English, we would tell them stories about the *foca* that's at the *playa*. We have quite a weird sense of humor in our home, and I made custom shirts with a seal on them that said, "Keep calm and *foca playa*." Sometimes we'd all come into the kitchen and see that we'd unknowingly decided to wear that same shirt on the same day. Thanks to their brothers, the Dedes also learned about the middle finger early on. Fortunately, they would give the pointer finger instead. Cue the Dedes middle finger shirt, caught on full display in paparazzi photos.

We call it Dede merch. We have hats and other shirts that say Dede terms like "*Yo quiero tu*" and "Dede middle finger!" showing a hand with the pointer finger raised, as Edu and Lu think this is the real middle finger. They will hold up their pointer fingers angrily and say: "*Foca playa!* I give you middle finger!" It's literally the best.

All good things have an expiration date, and our scheme started to backfire when I brought the kids to the Central Park Zoo. They saw the seals in the water and informed me that I

was completely wrong: the *focas* weren't on the *playa*! They were actually in the water in Central Park. Clearly, my children have inherited my tendency to process things in an extremely literal way. That was the beginning of the end of our amazing *foca playa* run, and now they clearly know, at three years old, that it's "fuck" and "bitch," or sometimes "fucking bitch"—or, Marilu's favorites, "bitchy bitch" and "stupid, tired bitch." (Where did she get that last one from???) I am unhappy but amused to announce that the Dedes have followed the great Baldwinito tradition of "Sharing is caring" and have shared all their bad word knowledge with baby Ilaria. So when she throws one of her "terrible twos" tantrums, I get a very clear "Bitch" chucked in my direction. Yay!

✳

New to motherhood, I was particularly conscious of my kids' diets. I was cautious of toxins, sugar, and artificial colors, and tried to avoid all chemicals. (My eleven-year-old daughter has now informed me that this is referred to as an "almond mom" and that it's totally "cringe" and "pick me.") I'm still semi like this, but I have loosened up a bit. My kids will eat Doritos sometimes and have an occasional soda. Not everything they eat is organic, and while most of our food is plant-based, they also occasionally eat things with unnatural ingredients. (I try not to dwell on it, because I'll spiral if I do.)

In our house, dinner is always a mix of fun, some chasing, some talking, and yes, some eating. But the more kids you have, the more opportunities for pickiness, and as you can imagine, with seven kids it's endless. I used to make gourmet meals for Carmen and Rafa, but then they hit that age when they woke up, and it was like, *That thing that I've been eating forever? I'll never eat it again.* Great. Thanks very much.

So now I just keep things simple, knowing that they all go through that phase. To accommodate them, every night we lay out a buffet with a few different things.

We're mostly plant-based at home, but our children will eat some fish and some dairy. My kids love tofu. If you start them on tofu early enough, they'll like it. We'll slice tofu, sauté it in olive oil, and put it on a plate. For other proteins, we'll get salmon fillets and just add some olive oil and lemon or some soy sauce and put them in the oven at 400 degrees until they're crispy. We also have Impossible Chicken Nuggets, or Impossible Burgers, or Smart Dogs, and the kids get to choose which one they want.

We'll cook different vegetables in the oven or the air fryer. They like green beans, asparagus, kale, and broccoli. Recently I've been making them salads, just mixed greens, cucumbers, and carrots.

Then we'll have grains, like an organic pasta. They love quinoa. I'll make it with vegetable stock instead of water, or a clove of garlic for some flavor. And they also like rice.

Every option is extremely easy to make. We'll put out a few, and the kids get to choose what to put on their plates, so they feel that they have a little bit of control over their eating habits. We also put out sauces. My kids love soy sauce, so we'll give them the low-sodium version. They also like nutritional yeast. Carmen loves shiitake sesame dressing.

Then they'll make bowls: a grain, a protein, and a vegetable.

We always have Taco Tuesdays, and we do it with Beyond Burger. Fridays are pizza night: super-greasy, delicious New York pizza. We also order sushi on Fridays. I'm always encouraging them to drink lots of water. Sometimes we do lemonade and water it down.

When I was a younger parent, I was reluctant to push them to eat certain things. But the gentle-parenting thing sometimes goes too far, where you're worried about their feelings about, say, broccoli. Like: *It's broccoli. It tastes good, it's good for you, eat the broccoli!* As with anything else, it just involves a little

patience. The answer is simple. Doing it is hard, but the answer is relatively simple.

When Carmen was little, we were at a two-year-old's birthday party. The mother who was hosting was beautiful and so cool and had the clear desire to make all those around her know she was above and beyond anything they could ever amount to. The kind of person who makes you feel like you might as well climb into a dark hole because you'll never be as beautiful or cool as her. In her presence, I always felt nervous: Why couldn't I be as breezy and stunning as she was?

Carmen's diet at that time was dairy-free (which was our choice, not because of an allergy). She rarely had sugar.

Unsurprisingly, typical toddler birthday, the menu at the party was pizza and cupcakes. This is now a Baldwinito special for birthdays, but back then my insides were reeling. I remember when I worked for *Extra*, I interviewed a mom, the creator of Organic Avenue, who told me that she brings homemade food to birthday parties so that her son will always eat well. I felt stuck somewhere in between: I thought, *Will something bad happen to my child if not everything she consumes is perfection, or should I be a laid-back parent who just wants her kids to be kids?* At this party I tried to remove the cheese from the pizza as nonchalantly as possible. Then the mom came up to me and said, "You aren't going to give Carmen a cupcake? Oh, right, you don't do the sugar thing . . ." Judgment, judgment, judgment. Which was I supposed to be? The mom who loved her child so much that not a single bite of non-nutrient-packed food went in her system? Or a cool and fun mom who was chill about it? Which mom group was I to fit in with? Which mom group was I to impress?

Instead of telling the truth, I pretended to be breezy and relaxed about it. "Of course she can!" I said. "Carmen eats cupcakes all the time. We love cupcakes!" (Meanwhile, my inner monologue was shouting: *Hilaria, shut up . . . Mayday! . . . Stop speaking!*)

I put a cupcake in front of Carmen and stood there casually, like we were expert cupcake eaters. The mother came over to me again, looking concerned. "Hilaria . . ."

"We love cupcakes!" I repeated to her.

"No, Hilaria . . . she is eating the cupcake paper. You need to remove the paper before giving her the cupcake!"

Sure enough, Carmen was chewing on the paper of the cupcake. I was so mortified, I wanted to crawl away and hide.

I continued to struggle with owning my parenting choices, and sometimes my flops, and trying to fit in over the years. Finally, I'd had enough. I've learned that I don't need to please everyone. I can just distance myself from people who make me feel bad, and do what I feel is right, even if I make mistakes.

When Carmen was nearly two and Rafa was only about two weeks old, we went to a friend's house for a Fourth of July party. Her house is gorgeous, right on the beach, and she is the kindest, most generous host. The food is always incredible, and the people are interesting, glamorous, and very fun. She has two older sons, and as a mother, she's been an inspiration to me.

That day, Alec and I were sitting outdoors on a cozy patio sofa in the beautiful afternoon light. Rafa was sleeping on my lap. I was still sore from giving birth and exhausted, especially because of Rafa's NICU experience. Carmen, a toddler, had recently learned the joys of bread. I mean she *loved* bread. Whenever she saw a breadbasket in a restaurant, she'd start shouting, "*PAN! PAN!!*" We used to beg the waiters to pass us the breadbasket under the table so that we could attempt to feed her other food before she filled up entirely on bread. I was working on trying to chill out a little and not be so strict about everything that went into her mouth. (Carmen laughs at me now, since her youngest sister had a lollipop before the age of one. She makes fun of "how far" I've come.)

On this particular afternoon Carmen was wearing a black-and-white-striped bathing suit, white sun hat, and pink sandals. She was gleefully running around the low outdoor coffee table, grabbing slice after slice of French baguette. When it got to slice five or so, I said to her in Spanish, "Carmen, would it be okay to stop eating bread until after dinner? Then, if you're still hungry, you can have more." She got upset with me, and the people nearby took notice. I repeated it in English because I was insecure and I didn't want people to think I was being mean. Now I couldn't care less: I have gotten very comfortable with the idea that my kids aren't always going to like what I say, but they know I come from a good place and have

a fair heart. Back then, however, my insecurities raged. I felt that what I was saying was reasonable and I just wanted to make sure Carmen ate well. She was getting visibly madder and madder. I was in that all-too-familiar place of trying to parent in public while my toddler very loudly let me know that she was pissed.

The self-consciousness and embarrassment crept in while I tried to stick to my messaging. Then a very famous actress interjected with "Oh, gosh! Children know what they should eat and are very in tune with their bodies, so trust their wisdom and let her eat bread!" She had spoken with such loftiness. Then she picked up the breadbasket and offered Carmen another piece. I became very quiet, stunned at being undermined in front of my daughter at the very moment I was trying to parent. Carmen slowly took a piece and ate it. I said nothing, heart pounding, feeling that if I put a stop to it, I would be seen as the bad guy by my child. After Carmen finished that piece, the actress, waiting nearby, said, "Carmen, would you like another piece of bread?" By this point, my toes were digging into Alec's legs, my just-given-birth hormones roiling, and I whispered to him, "Will you please take Carmen inside and I'll bring Rafa?" As I walked away, I defensively said to the actress, "I don't have a problem with her eating bread, I just want her to eat other things too. I don't want her to feel sick."

I silently fumed for the rest of the day, masking my feelings with smiles and nodding at people's small talk. As we left, I heard someone stumbling after us in the dark on the rock driveway. It was the actress, who was quite drunk. She slurred to us, "I gave your daughter so much bread. I hope she doesn't get a tummy ache!" I ignored her and kept walking away with my kids.

Later on, unpacking this with my friends, we thought of all the witty comebacks I could have said to her. I wished I'd been able to leave this woman schooled, with her mouth open. But over the years I realized that the real problem wasn't the bread or the potential tummy ache. The problem wasn't even that she'd gotten involved in a private mom-and-child moment. The problem was that *I* didn't have the confidence or know-how to stand up for what *I* felt was right. *I* gave my power away to her because *I* saw her as having a higher status. She was famous and beautiful and older than I was, with older children, and therefore more experienced. But besides that, I didn't have the confidence that my children would love me even if my choice was less fun than what someone else was offering. I should have looked the actress in the eye and thanked her for her experience, then removed my kids from her presence. But I was young and easily intimidated, and I honor where I was back then. I acted politely and maneuvered through a tough situation without throwing her off the balcony! Kidding.

The experience was a lesson in stepping into my self-confidence as a mother, and knowing that I must be the captain of my ship. I cannot try to fend off everyone with an opinion, but I can kindly filter their opinions when they come my way.

Your baby is your baby, and you get to trust your gut and make the choices that you feel are right when raising your child. Learning from each other is invaluable, but so many times it can feel pushy and like bullying. What are the cool moms doing? What if I don't dress my kid in the right way, wear my baby in the right way, have the right stroller, send them to the right school?

The best mom advice is often to just smile and nod and then do your own thing. It feels good to call people out occasionally, but nothing shows your strength better than just living, rooted to your beliefs, and not wasting your precious mind energy on them. Use it for fun things!

When one of my kids was three, they had a full-on tantrum about something they felt very strongly about: climbing into a New York City trash can.

It was December, and we were walking through the holiday market in Union Square. Alec and all the children were together. I was in my gentle parenting days then and tried to remain calm and collected as my three-year-old got progressively angrier with me because I would not let this very small person climb into the garbage. I saw so many judgmental eyes on me as my kid was kicking and screaming. I was sure they were whispering to each other, "That's Alec Baldwin's wife . . . what a terrible mother. No control over her child. Tsk, tsk."

All I could do was pick my toddler up, dodge the slaps and kicks, and march them home. I'd heard that the best thing to do was to let a kid throw a tantrum in a safe place, so I brought them into my bathroom and let them flail and kick as they said everything from "I hate everyone!" to "I want to go in the garbage!" to "I want to hit Florida." I filmed it so that I could get advice from my friends about what to do in this situation. Watching this video has become a favorite family pastime: all the Baldwinitos ask for it, as it's epically hilarious.

※

Leonardo is my third child, and we all agree he is the sweetest.

Knowing him at two and three years old, however, you would not believe that was possible, as he was a biter! And even though he was more than a year younger than Rafa, he was huge and would beat the living brother out of him. I had no idea what to do. I was so used to being able to explain

things calmly to Carmen and Rafa, and they would eventually listen. But when Leo turned two, he came in like a lion. I remember one time he bit Rafa on the lip, causing him to bleed. Rafa said, "Don't worry, it was just an accident!" Leo grinned and I flipped out. He was in that toddler phase of doing something wrong and then having zero remorse (though lots of evil laughter). It drove me nuts.

I tried various gentle parenting approaches like talking calmly and trying to reason with him. I asked friends and experts how to get him to stop biting. I would sit and explain to a two-year-old how we are peaceful in our family. I used all the right parenting words. (Now, looking back, I'm sure it just sounded like "Blah, blah, blah" to Leo).

I began doing time-outs and having him stay in a room alone for a handful of seconds. I would yell and try to intimidate him in a controlled way like an engineer putting a train into full gear and then slowing it down. This didn't work with Leo. I would sometimes actually lose my temper and feel badly afterward for yelling at him. Then someone told me that the most important thing was to stay consistent, model good behavior, hold him, and help him to calm his agitated nervous system. Also, that it would take time and patience. Phases come and go. This terrified me too. What if he just ended up bad and violent? I had much to learn as a parent.

The patient, consistent, firm-but-kind method worked. Leo has not only evolved into one of the kindest, gentlest, sweetest people I have ever met, but he is also wise and capable of helping his younger or older siblings through a rough moment or time. He knows the boiling passion that can result in exploding and hurting people, and he knows how to connect with them and calm them down. It is pretty inspiring to watch him teach others.

※

Recently, I was walking down the street in Manhattan with our youngest, two-year-old Ilaria. I was wearing a cute white dress, not at all a "mom" dress—meaning that if I bent over in it, my butt would show. We were only walking a friend to the subway a few blocks away, so I didn't bring the stroller. Ilaria was in the full phase of "me/*yo*"—needing to do everything herself, from putting on clothes to buckling seat belts to climbing into her high chair. She also decided that she absolutely must cross the street on her own—no holding hands. She currently refers to herself as "Baby Boss" (based on the animated movie of a similar name that Alec starred in), never Ilaria. You can imagine the battles that ensue on every New York City block. That day she started getting angry after we saw our friend off at the subway. By the time we had made it three blocks, she threw herself on the sidewalk after I had the audacity to forcibly hold her hand when crossing the busy street. I looked down to see she had her face buried in the nasty, dirty street, in between my equally dirty shoes.

I took a deep breath. She gazed up at me to see if I was going to break. I held strong, both of us stubborn, refusing to back down. I looked over at the pizza shop on the corner,

and there was a man I knew, watching me. Great. To my right, I saw some young girls, maybe in their early twenties, giggling and taking videos of this toddler meltdown that I learned later were posted on social media.

Hilaria, my inner monologue raged, *don't bend over and pick her up: the internet has seen your ass enough.*

(Side note: Right before our wedding, my dress blew up in a gust of wind. I was mortified. My father called me, angry, telling me my butt was seen all over Spain! I didn't think it could get worse until Alec decided to lift me up in a tea-length dress in Cannes when I was eight months pregnant with Carmen. Long story short, he didn't catch the bottom of the dress, which flew up, exposing my super-pregnant and less-than-cute bottom. On top of it, when I realized what was going on, I made an awful face. It made the front page of the next day's newspapers. Yeah . . . so, toddler on the nasty ground . . . I wasn't bending over.)

So I just stood there, waiting it out. I sent my thoughts and prayers to the girls who took the videos if they ever become mothers. And as for my acquaintance nearby, I just held my head up and existed in the moment, trying to find comfort in the discomfort of being stared at. Ilaria got over it in her own time and stood up. Alec was walking toward us, and we all stopped to say hello to the group we knew.

"How many kids do you guys have now?" the man asked.

"Seven," I responded.

"You had seven kids come out of you?"

That question again. You would think I would learn at some point. Just nod and smile . . . *Hilaria, just say yes! Or no! Or maybe a smile and change the subject?* Nope. Instead I blurted out the whole story, overexplaining—the live births, the miscarriages, the baby I had lost, all of it. As I did this, I was kicking myself internally. I rambled, my ADHD brain in overdrive. I could tell by the expression on the man's face that he didn't really want to know about all of this.

✳

People always ask me: What is life actually like with seven kids (and an Alec)? It's amazing and chaotic.

Right after this past Thanksgiving, my throat hurt a lot, and I could tell I had strep. So I went alone to an urgent care clinic and asked for a test. It was positive, of course. And the doctor's assistant said, "Usually, the adults we see with strep work with children. Are you a teacher?" I painfully and hoarsely muttered, "Well, I have seven kids! So sort of."

Because strep is contagious, I decided to bring everyone in to get tested. Cue seven children under the age of twelve and Alec Baldwin walking into an urgent care clinic in New York on the Sunday after Thanksgiving. As you can imagine, it was messy. Some of the kids sat on the floor screaming. Some were okay with that awful strep test. And some were . . . not good about it.

After all of that, miraculously, Romeo and I were the only ones who tested positive, so the doctor called in the antibiotics to a nearby pharmacy. By the time we left the clinic, Baby Boss was really mad. She was wearing little bunny shoes, and she'd kicked one off. So she just had one shoe on, and then she wouldn't put her jacket on, and it was freezing out.

My foot was broken, I was walking with a boot, and the three of us had to run over to the pharmacy because it was closing at 5:00 p.m. I clung to screaming Ilaria while sick Romeo trailed us, and we ended up getting there at 4:59. I told them our names and the woman said that my meds were ready but Romeo's weren't and they didn't have time to fill them. "We only have one more minute, so we're closing. Bye." She was so rude.

"But he's sick!" I pleaded. I asked if she could help transfer the prescription to a pharmacy that was still open, but she wasn't having it. She threateningly asked me if I didn't want my own antibiotics, in an effort to hurry me along. I paid for them and she immediately closed the electronic shade right in my face. I sat down in one of the chairs in the waiting area, seriously pissed. The baby, wearing one shoe, was taking things off the shelf and throwing them around. Romeo was sitting on the floor, miserable with his sore throat. I tried to call our doctor, but the answering service wasn't picking up. I just sat there, defeated but determined. Then my mom-resourcefulness came up with someone I could call and finally—finally!—I was able to reach a doctor, who transferred the prescription to a pharmacy uptown that stayed open later. I brought the kids home, then rushed up to the pharmacy in post-Thanksgiving traffic. The pharmacist there was so nice. He said, "Okay, we're going to try, but our machine for making kids' medicine is broken." I nearly collapsed right there. I said to him like a literal mad person with wild eyes and a whispering voice, "Please, please just try. I wish you so much luck." He looked at me oddly. I walked away to buy Motrin and Tylenol and water, because my throat was aching—also to not frighten the nice pharmacist more with my tired-and-sick-mom delirium of *I just want this medicine for my kid!* I guess my unfiltered weirdness was infectious because the pharmacist whooped and called me to the front. It worked! I could have hugged the man to thank him, but I remembered I had strep and was contagious. So I thanked him profusely from a distance, then walked the entire way home in the freezing cold to triumphantly give Romeo his medicine.

And then there's also the absolute hilarity of it all. Years ago we went to the beach in Amagansett on a beautiful day at the end of summer. I was very pregnant with Leo, and Rafa was only a baby. We were playing in the sand and Rafa was naked, without his diaper on. There were a few different families around, but it wasn't too crowded. Then suddenly we saw that Rafa was pooping on the beach. We were like, "Oh God, what do we do?" So Alec took a shovel and went and disposed of it. And Carmen took a tiny shovel and followed behind him, saying, "I got the rest of the poop!" And I thought, *Well, this is really kind of embarrassing, but he's a baby; it happens.* But when Alec walked back to our setup, we saw the people next to us glaring. And I realized that Alec had accidentally used their shovel to pick up our kid's poop. It was one of those shovels that you use for digging a hole for your umbrella. They obviously did not want it back. We tried to make it right by offering to buy them another one, but they were like, "No, we're good, thanks." Ugh, so sorry. Yikes!

I remember when Alec and I had Carmen: we thought, *Okay, this is the girl we make.* Then we had Rafa and thought,

RonShoots

And this is the boy we make. Although we raised them both from the beginning in conscious ways, I assumed I had much more influence over my children than I do. Having Leo a little over fourteen months after Rafa was a lesson in how two parents could make such different kids. I couldn't pin it on one being a girl and the other a boy. Leo was so different from Rafa, and then Romeo came and he was so different from all of them. These kids all bolted out into the world with their own personalities, spirits, and paths. I now believe it is my job as their mother to guide them but not force them. I have my rules, and I explain them lovingly but firmly. I tell them that I have eighteen good years to have them under my roof and to help them become good problem solvers, help them discover what makes them tick, and teach them to be kind.

I am a different mother to each of them, leading with the understanding that they are each unique. I am a partner to them all, but I must always respect that they will go further into the future than I will. A happy kid turns into a happy adult who can make a positive impact on the world. Or so I believe.

The more the years go by, the more I feel confident as a parent, and at the same time it's easier to accept that I'm going to mess up. Sometimes I'm overwhelmed with thoughts like *I don't know how I am going to guide them through whatever they're experiencing or help them figure out what direction to go in.* And I realize this is part of my life journey. There is truly no manual. I must just proceed with a good heart, my ego in check, and curiosity for what is to come.

4

CLICKBAIT

I grapple with the question: Why am I here in the public space? Why am I "relevant"? Am I here because an actor fell in love with me? Am I here because I'm a yoga teacher and have things to say about mental and physical health? Am I here because I had a lot of kids? Am I here because wild things have happened in my life and I'm good clickbait? I don't really know. I don't know if I am taken seriously or if I am a joke. Maybe it's both and all.

I am recognizable to people in certain contexts, but I can also walk around the city unnoticed and have the same freedom I had before I met Alec. No one looks twice at me or treats me any differently from anyone else, good or bad. A jostle here in the subway turnstiles, a friendly smile from someone when I hold the door, an annoyed New York City curmudgeon who feels I am in his way as we share the sidewalk, a guy randomly asking me out on the street (and who recoils at my response: "Sorry, I'm married with seven children, one stepdaughter, and a step-granddaughter!"). Single ladies, I told him I was so proud of him, though, for coming up to a woman in person. I hear about how sometimes online dating can be frustrating because no one meets like they used to. It's all online for many. I definitely frightened him after telling him I had so many kids, but then I encouraged him to be open and take a chance on people in person. Now that I think about it, I may have been the last person he'd ever randomly go up to, because I probably traumatized him!

Fame is a confusing concept. Does it just mean the sheer number of people who know about you or can recognize you? The *Cambridge Dictionary* defines fame as "the state of being known or talked about by many people, especially on account of notable achievements." What's a notable achievement anymore? My children love to poke fun at us and say that their parents are on the Y and Z lists of celebrities. Alec is Y; I am Z. And I'm fine with that—Alec, not so much.

❋

Before I met Alec, I'd seen only a few celebrities in passing. I walked by Harrison Ford on the street one time when I'd

just moved to New York, and I saw Susan Sarandon out and
about. One time, when I was living way out in Brooklyn, I
lost my phone. And then I heard this banging in the washing
machine: my phone was in the suds and totally dead. I sat
down and I cried and I cried, covered with detergent. It was
so expensive to get a new one, and I was a yoga teacher. When
I went to the Apple Store to get a new phone, I saw Salma
Hayek there with her husband. He's an extraordinarily successful man, and he's very elegant. And she is an icon, beautiful and talented. He was buying things for her, and she was
the adorable Salma, hugging him and thanking him. And I
looked at them, thinking, *I wonder what that's like. It's so easy
for them to buy something like a phone, and for me it's so difficult.* How funny that in the future I would marry someone
who has worked with her, and I would have the privilege of
getting to know her.

I honestly didn't realize how famous Alec was when we
met. I've struggled with whether to admit that here, because
now I realize that that sounds crazy. I hope that at this point
in this book, you've gotten to know me well enough to see that
I'm wired a little differently, and I hadn't focused much on
celebrity (and what comes with it). Of course, I knew he was
a well-known actor, but I don't think I really got it until after
we were married—what that all meant. Our wedding had been
swarmed by paparazzi, and at one point soon after, I turned
to a friend and said, "Wait, is Alec, like, super-famous?" She
looked at me, like, *How dumb are you?* and said dryly, "Well,
yes, he is."

The world of celebrity was also changing at that time: we were at the end of the more glamorous era and were moving into this world of social media, phones, and cancel culture, and everyone picking each other apart, famous and not. I wish I'd taken a crash course on how to date a famous person. Where were the *Princess Diaries* tutors when I met Alec? (One movie reference I know!)

At first, there was an excitement about being looked at and seen with him. There was an energy about it that was positive and thrilling. To say this is somewhat bold because of the negative connotation of being seen as a "fame whore" or an "attention seeker" (or a "star fucker," as I've been so nicely called). But there are amazing things that I've experienced through this world, and to deny that would be silly. To not admit that there is fun and excitement would be to lie.

Going to *SNL* is so much fun.

And the Cannes Film Festival is extremely glamorous. I've met incredible and incredibly fascinating people—actors, singers, politicians. I love music, and I remember meeting Ricky Martin and thinking, *This is so cool.* One of the most wonderful things about stepping into Alec's world has been being able to connect with people who do extraordinary things. It makes you kind of giddy: like, wow, I get to meet somebody who is so talented. I see it even with Alec. He'll get excited to meet or reconnect with people whom he really looks up to, like Paul McCartney, Jack Nicholson, Paul Simon, Audra McDonald, and somebody that we're closer with, like Lorne Michaels. I see Alec get starstruck, and it is so sweet.

So, yes, I'm grateful for the privilege of meeting these people.

But I come from a yoga world, where we are taught about the art of treating people equally. I believe that everyone is just as good as everyone else, no matter how much money they

have or how famous they are. I don't believe in hierarchy. And in the circle of fame, there's definitely a hierarchy. There are elements that can be quite toxic.

At the beginning of our relationship, I was baffled when certain people in the business and socialite circles wanted to meet me. I didn't understand why. Now, with perspective, I can see that I was getting sniffed out. I'd get invited to lunches and ladies' parties and I'd walk in thinking that maybe these women wanted to be my friends. No, Hilaria: this was business and social climbing. I did it badly and awkwardly. I had a few lunches with some very powerful socialites, and I imagine they were disappointed in meeting me, seeing that I didn't know how this transaction was supposed to work. I didn't know how to spend my days shopping, lunching, and "eventing"! I continued to teach yoga and focused on my close friends and family. I look back on this time lightheartedly. I had nothing to give and I am sure they just quickly moved on to the next. That said, I have also met amazing people who defy this stereotype of the "elite"—people who do want to just make friends and have meaningful relationships.

While I formed genuine friendships that I treasure, I've also gotten it wrong, thinking certain people were my friends. I think this is something that most women struggle with. *Who is my real friend?* One night Alec and I were invited to the house of a famous man and his wife for dinner. We'd been there before several times. The wife and I communicated often, and I felt close to her. Alec had something he had to host that night, so I told them that I would come without him.

I arrived and knew many people there and we were all having what I thought was a good time. Then the wife pulled me aside, looked me straight in the eye, and said, "We are only here because of our husbands. Let me give you some advice: If he doesn't come, you don't come . . . understand?"

I smiled weakly and didn't know how to react. I left shortly after, embarrassed. I told no one because I didn't want to misinterpret what had happened and perhaps cause unnecessary problems. But now I understand it quite well. It doesn't make me mad; it just allows me to see certain people for who they are and the system they play into.

I struggle with these kinds of people because I don't know how to play the game or become one of them. I don't want to. In the world of some fancy mom influencers, the talk is about yachts and the beautiful trips they take, cashmere here and diamonds there. Name-drop here and there and "love you lots!" When I tried to fit in with this group, it didn't matter what clothes I wore, or how many followers I had . . . my no-breakfast-at-Cartier ring . . . I just didn't belong as confidently and coolly as they did. I'd always come back to that insecurity, articulated so clearly that night by my former friend: I was only there because I was married to Alec. (I have never gotten that feeling from him. To Alec's credit, he is my biggest cheerleader and always includes me and respects me.)

Over the years, I've stopped caring about what these women think about me. When I'm having a popular moment, they want to invite me, and when I'm having an unpopular moment, they disappear. I'm now so comfortable with myself and how I move in the world and am proud that I've built authentic relationships. I've moved into a better place. I am not in a supporting role in my own life. I lean into good people I meet, both online and in person. I know what kind of community and group I came from. Why all of a sudden, because I married Alec, would I somehow know how to fit in with people who weren't interested in me before? I want to stick with my group, where I have common ground and feel safe.

Alec has a really horrible relationship with the tabloids.

He's an easy target: He lives with his heart on his sleeve and he also speaks up about abusive practices, sometimes in very straightforward ways. He's messy, he can be loud, and he'll say things he shouldn't because he's not thinking long-term. Unfortunately, tabloids and trashy news sites have a huge amount of power. People click on the articles even if they don't want to admit it. Private on our phones, right? Nothing is ever private. It's a booming business, and the more clicks these stories get, the more money the media companies make from advertising. It is a churning machine of collecting and thinking up and causing more drama to turn to clickbait and sell, sell, sell advertising. The entire enterprise becomes about negativity and vilifying certain people. I do see the noble side of Alec's defiance, but it's caused him and therefore his family a lot of pain by making enemies in the wrong places.

Alec taught me how to be a public person, but if I could go back again, I'm not sure I would have signed up for his Alec Baldwin master class on fame. But I fell in love with who I fell in love with, and one of my favorite things about Alec is that he hates toxic systems and will speak up. We are working on better ways to do this in our private moments together, but I think one of the reasons so many of us are drawn to him is how human and raw he can be. Alec is so connected to his feelings of right and wrong that he will react in ways that someone who has better self-preservation instincts might not.

And making enemies with powerful people is not a good idea. They hide behind the system, and he's on their list. So *I* get to be on their list! Yay! They don't care about right and wrong. It's about what sells and vendettas.

It was a big problem for these people that, as his partner, I seemed to soften his public profile. In the beginning, I tried to behave and be the good girl, but they came after me anyway. If I am portrayed as bad and fake and horrible, he loses his power yet again. This is a tactic as old as time: causing someone's wife pain is a tool of torture, a way of shaming and discrediting him. Women—we are such easy targets.

I remember stopping to chat with a famous TV personality one night at a restaurant. He, too, had been through a lot over the years—it seemed there was a problem with everyone and everything those days. We privately commiserated. I named a few people who I felt had been so cruel and how my instinct was to call them out. He cautioned me not to. He said that they believe they are "doing their jobs" within this toxic system and by responding to them I would be feeding into their hope for attention. They want me to respond because it gives oxygen to their trolling. It is perhaps one of the hardest lessons I've had to learn over the years: Say nothing. Do not respond.

There's a famous person, someone I've never met, who said nasty and untrue things about me and my family. It gutted me because I couldn't understand how someone could be so inherently cruel. How could she make up so much? Should I make a public response? I was alerted that her show was going to come out and what was in it. It felt like doomsday was approaching, and I became very sick with stress. Everyone I consulted said it was best to ignore her. I did, but it drove me up the wall. I went for a run the day the special was set to come out, my mind all over the place. Suddenly, *bam!*—I tripped and face-planted onto the cement. I got up sheepishly and kept on running, tears streaming down behind my sunglasses, and in my hyperfocus, I continued to run four miles more. When I got home, I realized I was covered in dirt, there was a rip in the knee of my pants, and I was bleeding down my leg—I was so upset that the physical pain hadn't even registered. I know it was a human response, and very much my neurodiverse response, but I was annoyed at myself for letting her get to me.

Her show came out, we didn't respond, and she even tried to bait me and Alec via Instagram. I imagine that she and her team were watching for a response from us, as this seemed to be part of the PR strategy for her show: make the Baldwins upset and get them to react, creating a news cycle and driving viewers to the show. We didn't engage with her and I guess I am proud of that. It made me mad at the system, but here, in this book, is where I can talk about it. I don't need to use her name and I don't want any problems with her, and I would like to be left out of any articles that mention her, because she has nothing to do with me. A total stranger. I don't need an apology for her derogatory remarks about my kids (they undoubtedly heard about them: I found one of my boys crying in bed, asking why this woman was making fun of him) or for outright lying about how she and I met.

Here's the truth: She did have the opportunity to meet me, years ago. Unbeknownst to me, we were at the same large event. Alec tried to introduce the two of us, and she made a face and refused. Alec told me the story afterward, and was upset by her rudeness. I defended her to him, saying, "Not everyone needs to meet me! It's fine." I have zero ego about things like this. This was an example of how Alec is good at reading people's character, and I naively always want to see the best in them. Even if I'm going to get it wrong sometimes, I still want to continue believing that people are good—she won't take that away from me.

I see her tag along publicly and stand up against bullying against women, and when I am weak, it drives me crazy, because it feels hypocritical. I don't like to say things about people I have never met, so I try to take a deep breath and let this anger go. When I am strong, I hope that when I see her leaning into good, it's genuine. No matter what, I hope I never meet her.

* * *

One particularly stressful time, paparazzi came onto my property and took pictures. It was totally illegal. The head of a famous tabloid had my phone number: in one of my attempts to figure out how to deal with this weirdness, I'd tried to make nice with him. He called me to say that they were going to run ugly articles about me anyway, so I might as well talk to him. I told him he was buying photos from people who had illegally trespassed, and he evilly said, "How can you prove that this blade of grass is your blade of grass in this photo?"

I hope you regard these stories as the stupid gossip they are. They are hard to talk about because this book, and anywhere else I share them, will result in press cycles that give steam to negative people. I feel a bit stuck, not knowing what to do. Do I stay silent, and not give them what they want? But then let them frame my narrative? Do I speak out and recklessly get drawn into their orbit? In taking this leap, will it be for the good of others who may be bullied and feel similarly to me? I hope speaking up is the next step forward. And please know that I don't want any of this to come off as whiny. Just straightforward.

When I first started meeting celebrities, Alec included, I noticed that many spoke about themselves in the third person. I was like, *What is this? Do these people think they're royalty or something?* I found it very weird. But over the past few years I've learned the purpose of this is to emotionally separate themselves from the overwhelming outside noise. When I allowed the public Hilaria Baldwin to mix with the private Hilaria, I lost my sense of real self. I am Hilaria. I am Hilaria to my family. I am Hilaria to my friends. I am Hilaria to my children. (Well, I'm actually "Mommy" to my children.) The person they speak about in the media is not always me. The point is, I'm a real person. And then there's a public image of me that has been distorted, both good and bad. That contradiction is very difficult to deal with, mentally and emotionally. It is this realization that has given me insight into this public-figure world that generations of people have been exposed to, whether they are the entertainer or the entertained. Gossip is gossip, regardless of how many eyes and ears are exposed to it. For a private person, it might not be the whole world watching, but it might be *their* whole world. This can be just as painful and overhwleming.

✳

When I started dating Alec, I received a call from an unknown number. I thought it was a friend of mine who was studying abroad and was surprised to hear a woman's voice on the other end announcing herself not by name but as a "reporter" for a particularly venomous publication. She said she "knew" I was "dating Alec Baldwin" and that she had some questions for me. I shakily told her I had nothing to say. She said something snide and hung up. Completely confused by this new experience, I called Alec and told him what had happened. He said I had handled it well. He also said that he wasn't hiding us from anyone and that they were bound to find out.

This was the first of a million such experiences. By this point, I've developed tools to handle it . . . better?

I had an enlightening experience with an actress when I was a TV correspondent for *Extra*. I did an interview with her at a film junket. Often, before an interview, I'd get briefed on people's boundaries, and the kinds of questions they will and won't answer. Sound controlling? Not really. It's the way celebrities attempt to set limits in a very invasive world.

I was told beforehand that I should not acknowledge that this actress was pregnant. Meanwhile, I waddled into the interview room, fully pregnant with Leo. The actress was beautiful and cozied her belly under a blanket draped across her lap. "OMG, you are pregnant!" the actress gushed to me. "Yes," robotic me answered, feeling my discomfort rise. She asked me everything from what gender my baby was to how I was feeling—the totally normal kind of conversation women have about pregnancies. All off tape—this is important. I gave quick and short answers, never acknowledging the actress's pregnancy, and directed the conversation to the movie we were there to talk about. The session ended and I thanked her for her time. She congratulated me and wished me well as I was leaving. Knowing that all cameras were off, I said, "You are being so nice and asking me about my pregnancy. I know you are pregnant, too, and I was told not to even acknowledge it, but I feel awkward because I don't want to be rude." She looked at me and smiled and just said, "Thank you for being respectful." My head spinning, I said goodbye and left. For years, I continued to think about this encounter.

I understand now that she was just trying to do what she thought was best to protect her family. She also wanted to talk about her career, and as a woman in Hollywood, the focus is so often on what you look like, what you're wearing, and your personal life. In contrast, reporters are much more likely to keep the focus on the actual work of male actors. That actress had every right to speak or not to speak about her family and her personal life. She had every right to be seen as a serious actress and keep the focus on her work. Her personal life is separate from her work. Saying it's fair game because she's noticeably pregnant is bullshit, and a justification for invasive behavior. Any woman who holds her own boundaries is an inspiration.

I saw this actress recently and brought this up. I told her it was a great lesson she gave in terms of limits we are allowed to set. She smiled and said, "Yes, it is all about consent." Learning that we can share ourselves in certain settings and hold boundaries in others has been a great gift to me. Our TLC show, *The Baldwins*, ended up being a safe space for consensual sharing, where as other experiences, like being chased by paparazzi, are invasive.

This is how the paparazzi work: a paparazzo takes a photo, their agency sells it to an outlet, the outlet passes it on to a writer, the writer's editor wraps it in clickbait, then it is distributed with ads. Our clicks fuel the fire; then the paparazzo goes back for more. Does it bother me? Yes. Do I think it's a toxic system that influences our culture and how we treat each other in our private communities? Yes. Does it lead to bullying? Yes. Is it harmful to children? Yes.

I have also seen that, no matter how much I or others speak out about it, it isn't changing. So as much as we experience this, I try to breathe and focus on what needs to be done to take care of my family and less on what I cannot control. It takes practice. I am not great at it yet, but I am always trying.

When I put myself in between the cameras and my family, it bothers the paparazzi. The storyline then characterizes me as "angry" or a "fame seeker": *Look at her—she loves to be in front of the camera!* The reality is that my husband is sometimes fragile and needs someone to stand up for him, my children are innocent, and I will not be intimidated.

There have been times when I have done physically reckless things to protect my family from these guys. I've chased down paparazzi's cars and put myself in between them and Alec so that he could get away. I prayed they wouldn't run me over. I am sure you may have had that mama-bear moment when you just can't help but protect your family. For some reason I think mothers are built this way. We may not always prevail, but we sure will be fiery in the process.

One time I strapped one of my babies into a front pack and set out while paparazzi waited for Alec outside our building. I walked past them and they began talking to me. I knew they would. I had a plan. I paused, took a deep, theatrical breath, and asked: "You want me to talk to you? You want me to talk to *you?*"—channeling my best Robert De Niro impression that I have seen Alec master over the years. Of course they nodded, in complete drooling disbelief at their luck that I would actually be stupid enough to give an interview to people standing outside my home during such a painful time. "Okay," I continued, "but not in front of my house, because that would be so disrespectful to my neighbors and just not right." When I spoke to them, I let myself look a little crazy and wild-eyed, which is probably why all these people think I am nuts.

I turned to walk toward the corner of our block, at the edge of the building, and stood with my back to the street so their backs would be to my door. They gathered around me, microphones outstretched, waiting with wide eyes and open mouths for whatever scoop I was about to give them that they could pass to their bosses. I took a long pause, checked on my baby in the front pack, and started saying the most nonsensical things I could think of. I had orchestrated a diversion and lured the paparazzi away from our front door so that Alec could escape unnoticed. As I watched Alec dart out of our building and into a car, I abruptly finished my rant. "In conclusion, I won't say anything to you!" Then I walked back to my building, leaving them utterly confused by my insane behavior. There were only two people who didn't fall for my idiotic trick: a cameraman across the street and a handsome on-camera reporter. These guys weren't the kind to follow Alec when he left. They would wait around and ask for an interview but not chase us. They saw the whole thing, probably laughing all the while. The reporter beamed a congratulatory smile and said, "Well played, Mrs. Baldwin, well played." I gave him a thumbs-up and high-fived the doorman on my way back in.

Hilaria 3, Paps 563,794,746,373,848. Whatever—I'll take the win.

In my continuing efforts to trick the paps, I have dressed up friends to resemble Alec to distract them so that he could get out of the house. I have taken Alec through shops and basements and out back doors to avoid cameramen. I try not to do the same trick twice, which is why I can discuss this here. I won't say which of my tricks I would try again . . . because I might need them!

One newsy morning I was all out of options and ideas. The entrances I had scoped out were closed and the paparazzi outside had cars, which meant they were more mobile and faster at following. Alec was supposed to go somewhere that had a glass front, and there would be no way to prevent them from following him and taking photos for hours while he was like a fish in a bowl. I didn't like how stressful that situation would be.

I got the kids off to school, and I went to go take my favorite barre class at Physique 57. As I was working out, my mind was far away—I was probably doing the left side on the right and not listening well—thinking up different diversions to get Alec out of the apartment. The best I could come up with was wearing something ridiculous and walking away from the building, similar to what I'd done with the baby in the front pack. I don't know how this craziness comes to my mind, and I don't know if it's brilliant or stupid or a waste of time, but for some reason I do it. I returned home, and as I stood in my closet, I decided it was between fishnets and a ball gown. The red ball gown at 10:00 a.m. might seem like a giveaway that I was up to something. Fishnets were insane enough in frigid weather, but tabloids love calling a woman an attention-seeking whore, so I put the stockings on. Lazy me also didn't want to fully change, and I figured I could keep on my T-shirt that I'd worn to the gym. I am a tired mom, and changing is exhausting sometimes. (Why are there no millennial laughing emoji faces in this book? The discomfort!)

I put on a short black skirt over the fishnets, kept on my She-Ra warrior princess shirt from my morning gym session, and threw on a silver leather jacket and big sunglasses.

Alec was waiting in the lobby for me.

"You look ridiculous, Hilaria," he said.

"I know. That's the point!" I said.

"This is such a waste of time," he said.

"It might be, but it's worth a shot," I reasoned. "I don't want to have to deal with any aftermath of them poking at you to get a reaction, even a small one. Then it's another news cycle. I give this about a 30 percent chance of working."

"You are shit at math, Hilaria."

Fair. But I was determined.

We called an Uber and took a deep breath and I walked outside casually, calling a friend on the phone. Slowly, I walked to the corner; it was working and they were following me. I giggled and laughed on the phone. My friend, oblivious to being a part of the plan, was like, "Hilaria, what the hell is wrong with you?" as I said random things such as "Oh, that's so nice!" and laughed, pretending I was having a casual conversation. I gazed up at the sky, looked around, and slowly turned toward the building to watch Alec dart into the Uber, then turned back around, freezing my butt off in that ridiculous outfit.

It worked! No one followed him!

I made my way back to my building and, once inside, jumped up and down in celebration with the building staff. We were high-fiving and then I went to sit on a heater in the lobby and gave them a play-by-play of my small triumph.

The next day I was in the papers as "Mob Boss Wife." I laughed along with them. Sometimes you have to.

✳

This is what I say to my kids about fame: "Daddy is an actor, which makes people recognize him and be interested in him. Daddy has also spoken up about broken systems that profit off hurting other people. Speaking up is the right thing to do, but that means we have some enemies. They do malicious things sometimes. We are always there to take care of our family." I don't say this to scare them, and I would love never to have these conversations. But kids are smart, and there's no way to hide from them what's happening with our family. (People have yelled awful things at them, and we've had to flee because of the press.) We go through all of it together. I try to find positives, and I think one is that we are a very close family, and our hard times have knitted us even more tightly together.

I am probably making a million parenting mistakes but I hope my children will always know that my intentions have been good, and I've always been focused on protecting them in this complicated world we live in.

Like most mothers, I am dealing with complex situations as thoughtfully as possible. You can only know what you know, when you know it, and try your best with whatever tools, thoughts, and energy you have in that moment.

I don't know what the right answer is. Is it better to be like those famous people who remain completely tight-lipped and controlled when it comes to talking about themselves? Maybe. Think about any famous woman. For years she may be tortured by the press. How many times will she allegedly be pregnant? How many times will she allegedly be depressed or whatever? Is it ever true? No! Well, who knows? The hope is that she continues to move forward amid all the ridiculous noise about her. It goes back to the fact that it's none of our business. Why can't we let women just be professionals? Why do we have to get involved and speculate over their personal lives?

The choice to do a reality show and to write this book was about showing what our life is. I didn't know what the experience of filming the show was going to be like, and I was very afraid to do it because I have heard only awful things about reality shows. You hear that they are fake and dramatic and that producers try to stir up drama to make better TV. I was also scared because we agreed to do the show at a very unstable time in our lives. I look back now and don't know what we were thinking. I don't think we were. It goes back to that same dilemma we always find ourselves in: people demand that we talk, but then we aren't supposed to talk, because when we do, every word will be picked apart and, regardless, we will lose.

This is the game bad people play. They don't want to know what's true or understand us. They want a show. A nasty show. We walked around for years doing our best to be silent. We spoke once by the side of a road after being chased for hours by paparazzi. We were with our children in the car and it got to be too much—too scary. These "journalists" don't care about what is decent and real. They care about causing drama and

RouShoots

getting paid. To be heard, when you are in a broken system, feels so cathartic.

We were in such survival mode, and so desperate for the truth to be heard, when we began our show. I think the show helped us through it. It felt like therapy, a diary of how we made it through every day trying to pretend to be happy for our children. People can take it or leave it. I have heard people say that we shouldn't ever be seen smiling or happy. I hope they know that we are in such pain and turmoil inside and we are using all our strength to keep our family intact.

I hope there will be people who watch the show and see our humanity and get a glimpse into our real lives. I am excited for it to come out and I am grateful to the amazing people who made it a very real and safe experience in which we felt comfortable opening up.

All I want when I see different cuts of the show—and edits of this book—is for it to feel authentic, for our kids to feel power in their story. If I have this, then it doesn't matter what the response is because I know what's real for me and my family. This show is truly our reality.

Throughout it all, I'm navigating this complex thing of *Where does my story end and my children's story begin?* When I tried to be more restrained and private when I first became a mother, it was even more toxic, more chaotic. I was told that, to lower the bounty that paparazzi are paid, I must share. There is a higher price for photos of celebrity children who are not seen very often. To lower this bounty, you can share images so that they become more common. I worry that some of my kids will look back and go, "Why did you do that? Why were our photos shared?" Some may agree with what I do and some may not. The best I can hope for is that there will be an understanding of my choices. I am trying to be true to us and to show our humanity to the world.

It is not just the images; it's the voice too. If you take away our voice, there's so much nastiness that can fill it. I want to teach my kids that they can hold their heads up high—that they can be proud of being Baldwins. It's an awkward dance we're doing, and I'm trying my best.

5

TRAGEDY

"I, Hilaria, take you, Alec, to be my lawful husband. To have and to hold from this day forward, for better or for worse, for richer or for poorer, in sickness and in health, until death do us part. I will love and honor you all the days of my life."

We don't have a crystal ball when we say these vows on our wedding day. Nothing can prepare us for how amazing and intoxicating the highs will be, and how heartbreaking some of the lows may be. We look forward to "for betters"—of having a family, making a home, following our dreams, walking a path together. But there will always be "for worse" in every single life and union, and not just grumpy days or frustration or the two of you not being on the same page. Those are more expected annoyances that, for me as a newly married twenty-eight-year-old, I knew we would get through with patience and work. The heartbreaking "for worse," the surprise "for worse," the scary "for worse"—there is no manual to prepare us or guide us through these deeply difficult and tragic times.

While Alec and I have experienced plenty of "for worse" moments, one tragedy stands alone: an accidental death that left a life lost, a son without a mother, a family broken, friends without their person, and an industry without a very talented and creative artist.

Our family will forever mourn the loss of Halyna. I have struggled for years to try to find the words to describe this devastating subject, and I have failed every single time. Because no words can capture such tragedy, such heartache, such emptiness, such torture.

That day, and the aftermath, are two stories that many people have tried to compound into one. The first is the tragedy of Halyna's death, which is not my story to tell. What I will speak about, the second, is separate, based on my own experiences as a wife and a mother.

The tabloid media will likely create headlines from this chapter. It's what they do. But I ask that we all have the decency to look beyond the headlines and remember what happened—someone died.

Have you ever ignored a call coming in from your husband? I did on October 21, 2021—actually, it was two calls. At that time, Marilu was my youngest, and I was taking photos of her. The phone rang and I ignored it. *I'm doing something right now*, I thought. Then Alec called again, which he often would do when he had a break from filming. We had already spoken multiple times that day, and I was planning to send him the pictures right after, and make a joke about how he was interrupting our photo session. He then texted me to call him right away and all of a sudden, my heart and my stomach smashed together: *Something must have happened.*

This conversation—and this entire day—was full of confusion, disbelief, pain, nausea, anger, fear, and heartache as the realization of what had occurred became clear over the course of many hours. I remember the loss, the distress, the beating of the walls and screaming and shaking. You may have seen images of my husband, doubled over in shocked grief, as photographers snapped photos and then outlets and newspapers purchased them to plaster around the globe. I tried to write a play-by-play of this day, and I've decided to omit it from this book, because I have seen from trying that all the emotions and chaos and gut-wrenching pain don't translate to ink and paper. They are more horrific than words can ever express.

"You are not alone, and I am with you," I repeated to Alec on that tragic night and beyond. "I will be here with you. I love you."

While Alec was processing what had happened along with Halyna's family and speaking with authorities, I was with our children in New York, and I knew I needed to rally the strength within myself to think clearly and make decisions for which I had no manual or previous life experience to pull from. I was told by mental health professionals that I needed to get Alec to a quiet place, once he could return to us, to try to prevent PTSD as best as one possibly could after such an awful trauma. I knew that the press was going to quickly swarm to my home, trying to get a glimpse of Alec's family and our reactions. I was facing the reality that there was no clear path as to where any of us should go. In a tragedy, there is no end goal, because it is all simply horrific. There is no way to make it better, because someone died. The only thing I could do was focus on my family. Nothing else mattered in the moment—no opinions, public or private. Just huddling in with the people who were truly involved. There was nothing more.

A friend who worked in the news industry came over that night and sat me down: "You need to get out of town, someplace the media won't expect. Alec is talking to law enforcement in Santa Fe. You need to take care of the children, so they aren't exposed to the nastiness they will experience outside your home," she counseled.

I left the house before the sun came up. I knew the longer I waited, the more press would show up outside. Standing in the lobby, I could see the lights of them all doing their intros and outros, waiting for me to come out.

I was greatly outnumbered and knew that as soon as I stepped out of our building, they could come after me. Unsure what I was doing, I put my hair in front of my face, waited until the majority of the reporters were speaking on cameras, and walked very slowly out the door. I took a deep breath and stoically put one foot in front of the other, staying close to the shadows of the urban buildings. My heart was beating

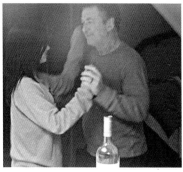

Alec and me.

Andreas Rentz / Getty Images

Pascal Le Segretain / Getty Images

Right: I've had so much fun dressing up over the years (even when my dress is so tight that I can't walk up the stairs and Alec has to carry me).

Virginia Mayo / AFP via Getty Images

Below: Our wedding at St. Patrick's Old Cathedral in New York City, 2012. I was so glad that my family was there to celebrate with us.
Mary Ellen Matthews

When I first joined Instagram, I struggled to understand its purpose. I decided that, as a yoga instructor, I would share pictures and teach yoga poses. What started as a fun activity turned stressful as I tried to outdo myself each day. But I posted every single day for 365 days!

I ended this series of Instagram posts with the best pose of all: an announcement of my second pregnancy.

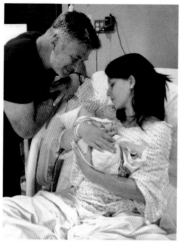

Alec and me with Carmen the day she was born.

Right: With my first pregnancy, I was nervous about how my body was changing, so I didn't take many photos of myself. But with my subsequent pregnancies, I got more comfortable and took more photos.

Alec and me looking at an early sonogram of Rafa, 2015.

Ireland was always so supportive of me when I was pregnant, and she loves her siblings.

When I found out that our third child, Leo, was a boy, I went and bought a blue teddy bear to surprise Alec. I think his face says it all!

Halloween is not just on October 31 for the Baldwinitos: us dressing up throughout the years.

"Boss Baby." Or as
Ilaria says, "Baby Boss."

Dimitrios Kambouris / Getty Images

*Jamie McCarthy / Getty Images
for Universal Pictures*

Me with my brother, my
nephew, and my dad while
visiting my family in Mallorca.
(Photo credit goes to my mom!)

My big brother came to
visit us in New York.

Carmen.
Alec Baldwin

Rafa at our rescue barn.

Edu (one half of
the Dedes).
RouShoots

Romeo. His name says it
all, right?

Leo presenting our new
puppy to Alec (who
knew nothing about
our buying a puppy!).

Baby Ilaria in the dress all my daughters
wore on their first birthday.

Marilu (the other half of the Dedes)
acting as Cindy-Lou Who, a
character from a Dr. Seuss book.

Carmen running down a
New York City street.

Baby Leo.

Carmen and Ireland.

Baby Rafa.

Baby Romeo.

Edu and Marilu, a.k.a. the Dedes. He
was so much bigger than her by the
time she was born.

Edu and Marilu pretending to
go to school.

Me and Leo.

Carmen and me.

My learning how to schlep
three kids around.

Me, Alec, Carmen,
and Rafa on the beach
in Amagansett, NY.

Me doing yoga on the beach
in Amagansett with Carmen
and Rafa.

Ireland and Carmen about
to roast their dad at an
event.

Rafa and Leo, when
they used to dress up
as the Backstreet Boys
and sing "I Want It
That Way."

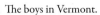
The boys in Vermont.

Romeo, Leo, and Rafa flexing their muscles.

Carmen and
Baby Ilaria in
Vermont.

Edu and Marilu, proud
of their gymnastic
accomplishments.

Rafa, Romeo, Leo, and Carmen.

Christmas 2022 in Vermont.

Carmen, Marilu, and Ilaria.

Rafa, Leo, Edu, Carmen, Romeo, and Marilu.

Me and Rafa.
RouShoots

Romeo's baptism.

Me and Ilaria.

Our dog (Macchiata), Ilaria, Leo, and Edu.

Alec and Romeo.

Alec and Rafa.

Me and the kids right after Marilu was born.

Rafa, Leo, Carmen, and me. I was pregnant with Romeo.

Me and the Dedes, one baby stacked on top of the other.

Edu and Alec.

Alec with Romeo, Leo, and Rafa after their respective sports games.

Alec and me heading off to an event. We took this photo before leaving and sent it to Ireland to congratulate her on the birth of her daughter. Look at all the excited aunts and uncles!

Leo, me, Romeo, Ireland, Carmen, Alec, and Rafa in LA.

The first day of school, 2024.

Us.
RouShoots

hard, but I kept my walking rhythm steady. *Eyes down, eyes down, eyes down*, I kept reminding myself. I have no idea how they didn't see me. I managed to walk down the street and all the way to the East Village, unnoticed. A friend drove to meet me there. Another friend put the Dedes in the double stroller, covered, and walked by the crowd unnoticed as well. No one followed her. I was sure that once they realized I was gone, they would leave my older children alone.

The plan was for me to find us somewhere to stay, and then the kids would join us later that afternoon. Eventually, Alec too. In the East Village, we got in the car: the Dedes and me. My friend asked me where to drive to. I had no clue where to go. This may seem silly, but it was one of those moments where I had that daunting feeling, realizing that I was the adult in the room. That I was to make choices for my family with no idea of what the right thing was.

"Drive north," I said.

So we did.

As we made our way, I decided that we should head to Vermont, where my grandparents had lived for a portion of their lives. They had both since died, but I knew that the town they'd spent time in was small, kind, and safe. I don't know exactly what drew me there. Maybe it was because none of my close family live in the United States now, and going somewhere that I had some family connection to would lend some spiritual support? To be honest, I don't know. I have tried to make sense of it in retrospect. Being a city person, I imagined that if you were to hide from paparazzi, it should be somewhere rural. Remembering as well that the trauma therapist had told me that Alec should be somewhere quiet.

We drove and drove, every so often stopping so I could nurse the Dedes. We arrived in the town I had vague memories of as a small child, and saw the roaring brook cascading over the rocks. Both my friend and I needed to use the bathroom. There are only two stores in the town, one of them a chocolate shop, which I remembered from when I was little. I opened the creaky door and saw a man organizing candies behind the counter.

"Can I help you?" he asked.

I walked over to him. Even though we were the only two people in the store, I spoke softly.

I told him who my grandfather was and that I hadn't been here for a long time.

This confession felt risky, given that I was on the run from the paparazzi. Would he recognize me and rat me out to the press? I don't know what I expected—maybe he would come around from behind the counter, and I would fall sobbing into his arms?

He looked me straight in the eye, and plainly said, "Sorry, I have no idea who that is."

I awkwardly changed course, my inner monologue berating me for once again blurting out weird things at inappropriate times. "Do you have a bathroom I could use?"

"There is a porta-potty outside," he said.

I thanked him and sheepishly walked out of the store.

As I searched online for a place to stay, our nanny was

driving my older children to Vermont, getting trailed by the paparazzi. In the past, the press wouldn't follow my children unless Alec or I was with them. This had been my plan: if Alec and I were gone, my children would be left alone. This time was different, as the paparazzi must have guessed that the children would lead them to me. The nanny kept driving, doubling back, circling certain areas to confuse them. Finally, after more than four hours, the paparazzi seemingly gave up and headed back to the city. We all united in a small cabin, hidden behind a thick row of bushes, that I'd rented for a few days, although I had no idea how long this would last. I was concerned about what kind of shape Alec would be in when he joined us.

After spending time with Halyna's family, Alec flew to Vermont and met us at the cabin. He arrived at night, after the kids were already asleep. He fell into my arms and sobbed, over and over, "How could this have happened?" I didn't know the answer to his question. I only knew to hold him and continue to say, "I love you, and you are not alone. I am here." We settled into bed, and one of our babies, sleeping in between us, stirred. Alec hugged him.

We eventually fell into one of those restless, tortured sleeps. And then, *bang!*

Alec screamed, jumped up, and began shaking.

Wide-eyed, I realized I had fallen asleep with my phone on the bed, and it had dropped onto the hardwood floor. I reached for him and told him it was okay. The realization that he wasn't ever going to be the same started to sink in. For the immediate future, from now on, I would need to take on the role of his protector.

Alec has expressed wanting to die many times over in the wake of this tragedy. He has voiced time and again that mental reeling when something so indescribably terrible happens: If there had to be an accident and a loss on that day, why wasn't it he who had died instead? He was diagnosed with PTSD. I have compassion and understanding for the unbearable pain that will forever live inside him. At the same time, I am his wife who so desperately wants him to *live*. This is a reality that I was not prepared or equipped for. I'm not sure anyone could be.

The paparazzi found us. We had gone to a local pizza place, and my understanding is that someone took a picture and called the press. I think that one of the biggest mistakes I made was thinking that a small town is a good place to hide from the tabloids. I have learned that one of the best things about small towns is that everyone knows each other, and everyone knows when something is off and different. *We* were the new, the off, and the different there. Ever since coming to this place that we hoped would be a refuge, I have learned to love a small-town community. As a city girl, I had to get an education in how to understand this kind of place.

News of the paparazzi chasing us around Vermont was blasted everywhere, and I don't feel like there is much to say about it. What you may not have seen were the locals standing up for us. One man put his pickup truck in between my car and a pap's car, trying to help us get away. An older woman knocked on our door and told me about a pap sleeping in a car by the local church, and together we essentially chased him away. She was wild then and must have been even wilder in her youth. We had people coming up to us and telling us how Vermonters (not Vermontonians, as I had originally thought they were called!) were expressing that we were welcome there, and they were going to protect us and take care of us. Another woman, just before Halloween, saw me in T.J.Maxx buying essentials and warmer clothes for my kids. She came up to me and said, "This might seem weird, but I feel like you need a friend." At this point, I got teary and welcomed her kindness. She invited us to spend Halloween with her in a nearby town, and the whole community was so kind. I am grateful to her and all the others because they gave me strength to parent and feign some joy for my children, when it all felt so dark and impossible.

I connected with a child therapist I knew because we needed to explain to our children what was going on. How do you explain something so devastating in an "age-appropriate" way? How do you explain something awful in a way that doesn't seem awful? Obviously impossible.

The therapist helped me with a "script," and I took notes on the sequence of how to have this conversation with our two oldest children. I was going to do it alone, because Alec was so broken. He insisted on being there, though, saying he wouldn't hide from his responsibilities as a parent. It was admirable but also heartbreaking to watch his pain during this conversation with our kids. I spoke to our children, asking questions like what their understanding of Daddy's job was. Their answer was along the lines of "Play pretend." Then I had to tell them that a horrible thing had happened, that someone made the set unsafe and someone died. Carmen was just eight and Rafa was six. I could tell that Rafa was too little to comprehend it—which informed me not to approach the subject at this time with their younger siblings. Carmen began to cry and said, "Why are you telling me this? I don't want to know this! I want to unknow this!"

We all did and still do. We all wish it had never happened.

As a parent, I have learned that tough topics become ongoing conversations as children grow. They process, think, have new questions. They hear things at school and in the news. They see their parents struggle and grieve. As the younger children get older, they too become aware and ask questions. As painful as this subject is, letting them know that they are welcome to talk—about anything, at any time—is what I am trying to do. We speak about it—its sadness and mourning a life tragically lost. There is no right way to do any of this.

After a few weeks in Vermont, we went back to our apartment in Manhattan. The press was still hounding us, but we needed to get the kids back to school. Alec continued to fall apart. I would walk into our bedroom and see him crumpled on the floor. I would find him sobbing alone. He was and is sensitive to loud noises, sudden movements, crowds, anything that feels too heavy on the nervous system. I started to see the world differently, protecting someone who was so fragile. Everything seemed dangerous.

Strangers would come up to us on the street with words of support—a blessing, a hug. We received so much kindness. Many actors reached out to check on Alec, and each expressed the stunned realization that this could have happened to any one of them. They were telling this to me, but I knew they were also telling this to themselves.

The media was vicious and relentless. The day after Alec was first criminally charged, I stood downstairs in the lobby, talking to the doorman, who, after so many years, is like family now. The press crowded by our front entrance.

"*Mija, no salgas.*" *Don't go out*, the doorman begged me.

"I am going to ignore them, march past them, and walk across the street and order a coffee, just like I have every right to do," I said in one of my determined-yet-totally-knowing-this-was-a-bad-idea moments.

Our doorman Joey looked at me, like, *You stubborn little crazy person*, and reluctantly opened the door. I set out with dread yet trying very hard to seem courageous. Maybe it would be okay?

Nope. Big mistake.

I got swarmed. I had to cover my head and beg the paparazzi to give me space. Scared of being crushed, I suddenly felt an arm around my back, and before I knew it, I was being lifted across the street, straight into the tiny coffee shop. I opened my eyes and saw that it was Jason, our building's super, who'd helped me. We stared at each other, catching our breath. I sheepishly looked at him, but then I resumed my pretend toughness and noticed the shop's door was still propped open.

The press was craning through, and I walked with feigned confidence over to lift the doorstop and have it shut in their faces. I turned my back to the windowed storefront and faced the barista.

"Want a coffee?" I asked the super, trying not to show that I was shaking.

✳

The wickedness that ensued over the following year was a constant roller coaster. In the wake of the initial prosecution misconduct, Alec's criminal charges were temporarily dropped. I found myself back in the lobby, next to Joey the doorman, determined to learn from the last pap-crowd fiasco.

"How many of them are out there?" I asked.

"Not one," Joey said.

I was unsurprised at the hypocrisy of it. The circus of press when Alec was charged, and now complete silence outside our apartment when they dropped the charges. Joey happily opened the door to the peaceful street, and I walked undisturbed to get my coffee. The barista pointed it out before I could: "Wow, what a lesson in humanity."

Over nearly three years there were downs and reprieves, but never ups, because there are never ups from tragedy. These waves tortured Alec, and he became a completely different man, seeming to break more and more each day.

I have not wanted to speak about how these years have taken a toll on his health because I was so terrified of being told that I was trying to gain sympathy or getting accused of making it up to victimize ourselves.

I have grown and am tougher now and have gotten to a point in life where I feel I have more strength, and I won't let toxic systems and bad people manipulate or frighten me. They can say what they want to say. I have zero control over this, but I do have control over what I allow to filter in, and my response is to not let negativity alter my voice and presence.

The first time Alec passed out, he was sitting at the kitchen table, the Dedes on his lap, surrounded by our other kids. Suddenly, his head flopped back, and his eyes rolled toward the back of his head. My children screamed, and I ran toward him, shouting for the kids to leave the room. I stood on the bench, looking down at him, shaking him and shouting his name for what felt like an eternity.

Finally, he came to, and I brought him to the hospital. They said the stress of the situation was affecting his heart.

I was so angry at how Alec was being treated by the legal system. What the prosecutors were doing had real consequences on his life. I could understand if it was in the pursuit of justice, but it was blatantly not so, as they had already shown their true intentions with their own words and actions.

On a Friday in March 2023, Alec's health quickly declined. His hands became cold, and he could barely walk. I brought him to the emergency room. They did many tests. It was more stress, the doctors said. We went home and I tried to get him hydrated. He essentially stopped eating and drinking. It was like he was turning off. Over that weekend, he refused to get off the couch, and insisted that he just needed to sleep. He has a way of doing this in such a cranky manner, a tactic that he knows will get me to leave him alone on most occasions. We spent the weekend like this: me pestering him to eat and drink, him shooing me away.

On Monday morning, I took the kids to school. I got a message from our nanny saying that I needed to come home because Alec was really sick. I rushed back and found him shaking, unable to stand up. He still refused to see the doctor, doing his best Alec-curmudgeon again to make me leave him alone.

The women who work with us in our home are some of the most inspiring people I've ever met and they have guided me through so much. They possess the perfect mix of wisdom and toughness. Despite Alec's protests, we all weren't going to take no for an answer. Together we fought back his whining and determination to just lie on the couch without seeking help. Not this time, Alec. Socks, shoes, jacket. We got him on his feet. He was weak and fell back onto the couch, unable to walk, and we weren't strong enough to get him down to the car. He begged for no ambulance because he didn't want it to attract any press. I texted two people who work in the building to come help. Alec resisted as best he could, but we finally were able to get him into the car and off to the hospital.

He drifted in and out of sleep in the car, but I felt he had perked up a little. When we arrived, I came around to his side to help him out. Alec, who is over six feet tall to my barely five foot three, started saying to me, "You are blocking my vision."

I have a tendency to hyperfocus on things that plainly make no sense and understand everything through a very literal filter, so I argued that this would be technically impossible due to our height difference.

Then Alec slumped back, eyes rolling, mouth open. I began to scream, "Help me! Help me!" All of a sudden, our quiet operation of getting him to the doctor turned into his being slumped in my arms and me screaming. I don't know how I held him up. I also don't know how New York was so quiet, with no one to call for on a Monday morning.

Mikey, our driver, ran inside the hospital to get help. I was sure Alec was dead. I thought I was going to vomit from feeling so helpless and heartbroken. *How could this be happening?*

The amazing hospital staff ran out, buzzing around him, quickly hooking him up to IVs and monitors. Thankfully, he was alive. But he didn't wake up for a long time, and when he did, he couldn't walk or remember much. It was spring break for the kids, and so I toggled between going home to care for them and rushing to the hospital to be with Alec throughout the day. Baby Ilaria was six months old, and I was nursing her. I would bring my pump in a backpack everywhere.

Alec was in the hospital for more than a week, and when he left, he still couldn't walk without the help of a walker. Shortly thereafter, he was scheduled to go finish filming *Rust* in Montana.

I feared if the world found out he was unwell, it might complicate an already complicated endeavor to finish the movie. So to disguise the situation, I bought an orthopedic boot, the kind you wear when you break an ankle or a foot, and I put it on him before we arrived home in an Uber. And when he went outside he walked with a walker and the boot, until we could get him stronger again. The media assumed he had broken something and was recovering. When he would leave the apartment, I had to remember to put the boot on the correct foot!

Shortly afterward, he left to finish filming the movie. He was still weak. The press made fun of him for his horseback riding. Alec has now had two hip replacement surgeries, and the filming was just before he had his second one. After he finished the movie and could finally get the surgery, his hip socket was so bone on bone that they had to take the hip out in pieces. I wanted to beg these awful people who were reporting on him cruelly, "Do you know what this man has been through while trying so hard to rally, show up, and do his job, masking what is really going on?"

In all fairness, they didn't, and yet it's quite possible they wouldn't have cared even if they did. Some people are just wired differently.

✳

The morning that Alec left to go to trial in Santa Fe, Carmen woke up all her siblings to say goodbye. She had asked me during the week before, "When I say goodbye to Daddy, do I have to say goodbye to him in a special way? Like goodbye for a long time?" I have learned that the best way with my children is almost always the most straightforward. They have seen such dark things and to tell them "It's okay" all the time will eventually lead to them not trusting me. "Yes, you do," I told her honestly. They had to know that when they said goodbye to their dad, it could be for eighteen months if he were to be found guilty.

I struggled with my wish to keep my whole family together during this time. I initially wanted to bring all my children to Santa Fe, but it was so complicated, and I was afraid it would be seen as me using them for sympathy. Eventually I decided to bring only Carmen and the baby, Ilaria. I felt like a terrible mother because I couldn't bring all my kids, but Carmen wasn't in day camp, and the other children had a routine to be kept occupied by. Carmen wanted to come—she thought she'd be less scared if she could be there with us. Who knows if I got any of this right. It was the first time I was away from my children, besides going into the hospital to have another baby.

During Alec's trial, I sat directly behind him, on the right side of the courtroom. The left side of the courtroom was full of reporters and photographers. Much of the press had their cameras trained directly on us the entire time. For the most part, I refused to show emotion. I didn't want to give anything to these people. Toward the end of the trial, though, it became more and more difficult for me to hold it in.

There were times when Alec came to speak with me, just to get a moment of connection, or to ask how the kids were doing, or to tell me something. When we would go near each other, the cameras went at us harder. I would put my hand by his face to cover our conversation, to prevent any type of lip-reading scenario.

Months later, my friends and I became oddly obsessed with this lawyer online who breaks down legal cases. She is funny and smart, and we all enjoyed watching her. She is open about her ADHD and dyslexia, and I find her to be very courageous and inspiring. The way she speaks is busy and all over the place sometimes, and I see this in myself. You may even see it in this book. When she spoke about me and Alec, it felt clear that she didn't like us, particularly me, whom she referred to only as "Alec Baldwin's wife." It hurt my feelings, but what else was she supposed to believe when there was no reason given to see my humanity because of misinformation from tabloids?

At one point in an episode, she said, "I don't want to watch Alec Baldwin's wife petting his face again!" I wish she could know what I was juggling, sitting there and trying to be a human, a wife, a mom, and a friend, while also being sitting clickbait. That "petting" of the face was to block our conversation from the cameras.

I've learned to do what needs to be done, and to ignore the noise in order to protect my loved ones. I oftentimes don't know what I am doing, but I do know that I will throw myself to the character-assassinating wolves to protect Alec and my kids. Call me crazy? Go ahead, it's happened so many times that there is no point in stopping now. I have to put my morals before my reputation and ego. My friends, consoling me from time to time when I have the vulnerability to show how hard it is, help lend perspective and, most importantly, remind me to laugh and to try to find the joy in things when it all becomes too much.

Weeks after returning from Santa Fe, I walked into a favorite shop of mine in New York. The owner came up to me and embraced me. "I am so glad it's over," he said. "They've tortured your family for years."

My eyes stung with tears. To hear those words—"it's over"—felt like such a relief and so painful at the same time. How do you know how to live after "it's over"? For so long, our family has existed with a constant baseline of paralyzing awfulness and uncertainty.

People continue to ask me if I feel relieved, if Alec feels relieved. As if all of a sudden, it's just better. I don't know how to answer that other than to say that it felt like we were carrying a huge boulder. And now we're allowed to drop it. But our arms still hurt and will continue to for a very long time. Maybe forever.

I've learned that more than one person's pain can be valid. No pain should be viewed in comparison to any other. Pain can coexist. There is unfortunately no pain limit in this world, and it's not something we should rank or judge, nor should we question another's experience when it comes to grief or distress. To feel pain is to be human. By documenting my husband's pain, I do not take away from anyone else's. It's just what it is.

Many people don't seem to stand up for each other anymore. The world is so fear-based. If a person has any sort of strike against them, people run the other way and ostracize them, cancel them. I could have left Alec. I could have taken our kids with me and abandoned him. But I didn't. I stood by him because it was the right thing to do. I saw and know the truth.

For anyone who has experienced tragedy, the question is: How do you move forward? Alec and I tell each other that it will take a while to find whatever we are supposed to look for in our future. We don't know for certain what it looks like, and it is not going to happen quickly. It will never not hurt. We are not the same people as before, not the same couple. Who knows what we will find and how we will learn to be. Every day, we get up and do our best to parent, partner, grow, and find our way.

6

DIFFERENT, NOT SO DIFFERENT

I've been told I was different for my entire life. I got diagnosed with ADHD as a young child, when it was something to be embarrassed about—a nasty mark on your intelligence. As a student, I was very insecure. When we had to read aloud in class, I would count the people in front of me to figure out which paragraph I was supposed to read and then I'd try to focus on it until it was my turn, hoping to sound like the other kids. Often I'd chicken out and excuse myself to the bathroom. When I worked for *Extra*, I would try to get my questions and lines as early as possible and attempt to memorize them. Reading off the prompter was so hard for me. My eyes would jump from here to there. When I read, the black of the letters look less bright than the white of the page. (You can imagine how much fun it has been to write this book. Bless the copy editors.) I choose now to laugh rather than feel shame in how a word sends my mind spinning into a thought that has nothing to do with what I am reading. I'd stutter, get lost, get embarrassed. Now I find power in owning it. Alec calls it "squirrel." There's nothing like humor to heal our insecurities.

When I was ignoring the fact that I was neurodivergent, I tried to remedy my symptoms the way I assumed a "normal" person might. Can't read? Get glasses. Can't comprehend? Maybe I need hearing aids! The optometrists always had a difficult time figuring out my prescription. Over the course of nearly thirty years, I've tried so many different glasses, but none of them helped me to read aloud better. Eventually, I came to terms with the fact that it was my ADHD, not my eyes. My difficulty in reading is in the processing of my brain, which makes it hard to focus.

Similarly, a couple of years ago, I started to worry that I was losing my hearing. Sometimes when people speak to me, I can't understand what they are saying. English, Spanish . . . the language of movement. It didn't matter. I would see their mouths moving but nothing registered. I never order the specials at restaurants because I can't understand what the servers are saying to me; classroom lectures were like Charlie Brown's teacher talking: "Wah wah wah wah wah." How many times do people have to say my name to get my attention? *Hilaria?*

Hilaria! My kids even know to make eye contact with me when they speak to me. Rather than understanding that this is a comprehension issue, I was sure I just couldn't hear. It had to be why I was forgetting things and having trouble comprehending things. Terrified, I went to get a hearing test. In the booth, I was instructed to say yes every time I heard a beep. The test couldn't have been more than five or ten minutes. When I came out, the technician said, "You have perfect hearing, but you aren't taking in the information. You can hear; you just aren't comprehending. Add two languages on top of that, you're a tired mother of seven, you're stressed, you have a lot on your plate. But your ears work perfectly."

This was the moment when I chose to finally learn more about my ADHD and dyslexia rather than to just attempt to fit in. I discovered that so much of how I am different and how I have struggled to be "normal" was due to ADHD and dyslexia, plus being bilingual on top of that. It really sank in that forgetting words is normal in a monolingual brain but more common in bilingual and multilingual brains. Add ADHD, and it's a whole distracting, code-switching mess. Learning this gave me understanding and compassion for how I am wired. It made me stop hating parts of myself. And it made me stop feeling like I was broken.

When one of our sons was diagnosed with ADHD, I took it hard. They say it is genetic, so I felt like it was my fault; I didn't even want to tell him. But it's funny, because he knew: he kept telling me he had ADHD long before we tested him. I dismissed it, since kids talk about ADHD these days, and I thought he wanted to be like some of his friends. I do love that although in my day it was shameful, now it's less so. I didn't want to think about my son suffering and struggling as I had done. When I think about how I withdrew from people, was laughed at, still get laughed at . . . I never want him to hurt like that.

He's had sad moments: when he heartbreakingly called himself stupid, it reminded me of my own childhood, when I wrestled with the same feelings. But my stubborn determination overtook my guilt and fear. I got on my phone and together we looked up the positive aspects of ADHD: creativity, resilience, hyperfocus, spontaneity, humor, high energy. We sat there and went down a rabbit hole of amazing videos that made us laugh and realize things about how we function, and how much the world has changed for the better since I was a kid. The traits we learned about resonated with me, and I began to think that perhaps it's not that there's something wrong with us but rather that the world isn't set up for how our minds work.

Empowering my son with this, teaching him the upsides of his diagnosis and not just the limitations, and working on the harder parts together has made us proud of how we are wired. We always strive to improve in all things, not just as it relates to our ADHD. We are forgiving when we forget or get distracted. We understand that maybe we need a certain routine or activities or breaks.

For us, this might mean working a little harder in conventional learning situations than those who don't have ADHD. Put us in an environment that works for us and watch our brains fly. I try to make it a superpower for him, knowing too well from my own experience how hard the journey can be. So much of what I am learning in this life is about questioning all types of systems and asking why things have to be a certain way. So many of our shoulds and shouldn'ts are just made-up rules. Breaking away from them in some areas of our lives can be very freeing.

My parents raised me and my brother within an untidy mix of cultures, languages, and international formative experiences. My mom was a student and a medical resident for much of my childhood, then eventually a doctor, and my father had quite a few different jobs. Our home languages were both Spanish and English and the one rule was: if you start a sentence in a certain language, you must finish it in that same language. It was a way to speak the languages well. My brother and I were rebels, however, and would secretly throw in words here and there, mixing both and resulting in Spanglish or espanglés. As adults, we speak to each other in Spanish nearly all the time but still will incorporate some English. See, this is how it works when you are bilingual and beyond: it's all in your mind and sometimes the barriers break. It's so much easier communicating with other people who just understand all of it; you can be freer and messier. Because of my ADHD and dyslexia, I've always struggled with going back and forth between the two languages; I get stuck, distracted, and forgetful.

Wherever we went, my brother and I were often the odd ones. In Spain, we were ambiguous and were always having to explain that we weren't born there. When we were in America, people would point out the Spanish influence on our language and mannerisms. Humans are wired to spot the differences, which meant nothing about us could easily be defined. We were always different and lived in a state of not really belonging anywhere.

Growing up, this wasn't something people talked about. You were supposed to get in line, figure it out, and fit in by osmosis. My brother reacted by becoming extremely shy and throwing himself into the Spanish side of our upbringing. He married his Spanish wife and has lived most of his life in Spain with her and their son. As for me, I got to New York as soon as I could, knowing that it was the land of not belonging—and therefore belonging completely.

I chose to attend New York University for my higher education partly because I wanted as straightforward a college experience as I could get. I wanted the big classes and the urban environment that would allow me to blend in so that maybe no one would notice the discomfort within me. I thought that maybe my learning differences could be cured by immersing myself in a traditional education system and maybe I would magically become like the neurotypical students. I didn't understand that this was what I was doing back then, but it is clear to me now that it was an attempt to "fix" my "broken" brain, as I used to think of it. Unsurprisingly, I struggled, even though I got good grades. I was interested in becoming a doctor and began taking the giant premed classes, but everyone else just seemed to get things much easier than I did. No matter how hard I tried, I couldn't keep up. So I shifted to the smaller classes in art history and wandered around museums, writing papers on tangible things in front of me. I found my way—tripping, falling—but eventually standing up again and continuing on. I didn't have friends in college because I was so busy. I worked and studied, had an eating disorder, and it was a hard time for me.

My brother and I don't get to see each other very often because of the physical distance between us, but we talk frequently.

Years ago, during one of our hour-long chats, we mused

about what makes us so different and where we belong. He lives a private life, so his mixture makes him fit right in with the billions of other people who speak more than one language and have a little bit of this and a little bit of that cultural upbringing or adulthood.

It's normal and pretty uneventful, but, for me, living in the public eye, these same traits have provoked people to pick me apart and "play make-believe" with my identity and life. I look up to my big brother; he's always soothed my insecurities. That day on the phone, we agreed on something: we were chameleons. I see this term hurled at people as an insult, but I think it's actually a superpower. My brother and I have become so flexible, so attuned to our surroundings, that we've adapted to and evolved in whatever community we've made our home.

While being a chameleon isn't a bad thing, certain people see it as something negative or confusing, preferring to sniff someone out, box them up, and glue that box shut so they don't have to try to figure them out ever again. Like, *I've figured you out and left you right there! Stay put!* Those who code switch and have a wide bandwidth to express themselves in different situations and with different communities threaten some people's primitive, animal instincts. They shouldn't, because language and mannerisms are just a way to express our thoughts. These don't necessarily change based on the language we're speaking.

I believe that everyone is morphing all the time—in behavior, speech, the way they dress—based on their surroundings. For most people, it's a more subtle shift and therefore more socially acceptable. It is our job to come into this life and evolve. How can we not? Every experience, good or bad, changes us if we are curious and let people in.

During Covid, Alec brought us to see his hometown in Massapequa, Long Island. It was fascinating to me because it was such a traditional American place to grow up, with its ball fields and schools, the local milkshake spot and pizza hangout, the community center. He even showed me the "Dog Doo Island"—the place everyone walked their dogs in the morning to relieve themselves. He knew the names of his neighbors and told us stories of balls thrown through windows, bike rides, stitches, and first dates.

While I'd had my own experience growing up in Boston, I couldn't tell you the name of one neighbor. We were always in and out, back and forth, and never felt settled for very long. We always had a revolving door of people coming in and staying with us from all over the world. I think this has given me a complex relationship with the word "home."

When I was little, I would tell people that I belonged in the middle of the Atlantic Ocean, between the United States and Spain. When I am here, I long for there, and when I am there, I yearn for here. It's a beautiful thing to speak multiple languages and to intimately know more than one country, but it also comes with the pain of never feeling quite complete. And I probably never will. I still do not know where home is. For sure, it is with Alec and my children, but I don't have a specific place. I love New York and have lived here longer than I have lived anywhere else. I miss my family in Spain and the traditional culture of food, music, and dance that my family instilled in me.

I've always wondered what it would be like to just belong. My father called me once when I was going through a particularly hard time and said, "I'm sorry I brought you up in such a complicated way." He himself had a pretty international upbringing, with many influences, and the more I learn about my background, the more I realize that many of us have moved around a lot. I told him I was forever grateful for the experiences he gave me and to never regret anything.

Alec and I are doing something similar with our children, and it's something I stand by fiercely. In our home, just like when I was growing up, we turn to one person and speak in Spanish, then to the next and finish in English. Do we forget words? All the time. Do we mix and mess things up? Yes. And guess what? We know it is normal and it makes us laugh. This is truly a positive thing. There are countless memes online about multilingual flops, and they are taken as normal and happy and funny. It goes back to my mom's wisdom: "Is this a problem with Hilaria or Hilaria Baldwin?" Definitely Baldwin. I obviously cannot stop people from saying awful things, but I can attempt to stop the things they say from filtering down to me and block them out. I don't want to play the same game by different rules simply because I am a woman and I married Alec.

People are always evolving, and cultures are fluid. Some do it as consciously as Alexander Rae Baldwin, a.k.a. Xander Baldwin, who went to Hollywood and became Alec Baldwin. Alec worked hard to lose his Long Island accent, eventually becoming a world-famous voice actor, and he is celebrated for this evolution. I watch TV clips of myself when I was younger and I sound different than I do now. People's accents change based on who they surround themselves with and where they live. When I was in my twenties, I was mostly around bilingual people, and we generally were discussing yoga or fitness. The language of movement is a completely different one, filled with sounds and rhythms and sentences that are not proper in any language anyone may speak. That's not my life now. As I wrote earlier, I've taken great pains to learn how to speak more clearly as a result of being picked apart. I've had speech therapy and I have worked very hard with doctors and therapists on my ADHD and dyslexia, which comes through especially when I speak. I think I have polished up the way I talk a bit; I just feel wary that I chose to try to change because of negativity. I still code switch, and the sound of my voice still has quite a spectrum, depending on who I am talking to, how tired I am, if I am mad or happy. It's normal. And I am trying to gain confidence and be more joyful about it. Own it. I always say I speak a language of "more or less" (*mas o menos*). I get close to what I mean and then hopefully one can figure out what I am talking about! I truly don't have the energy anymore to do any differently.

I see my children communicating very similarly, living in a multilingual home and being bilingual themselves. They can switch languages easily and can identify who to speak to in each language. They also struggle sometimes, and we all laugh and look up a word that has slipped our minds. Thank goodness for Google! The best part is that in New York City they are exposed to so many different kinds of Spanish. For those who lump all Spanish together: Don't. Just like English-speaking countries, Spanish-speaking countries differ in accent and words, which even vary within a single country. Living here for so long, my Spanish has gotten so mixed because I have adopted many different words from different places.

When I was a child, I once asked a monolingual American woman, a friend of the family, to read me a book. It was *La Bella Durmiente—Sleeping Beauty.* I showed it to her, excited about story time, and she said, "I can't read this book . . . it's in Spanish." I vividly remember the confusion I felt. I thought all grown-ups could read!

I see now, after raising my own bilingual children, that when you're young, words and sentences just make sense; there is no separation between Spanish and English in their minds. It's fun to see each one have the aha moment when they realize that this isn't the case for everyone and the words that they know are actually two completely different languages. It makes me sad sometimes that some people can't marvel at how the human brain works for language and instead shame us. Not just with me, but with so many, in so many different ways.

As much as I love the term "code switch," I don't think it's so much of a switch as a blend. It's not such a conscious thing; it just happens. Once, when Carmen was little, she whispered to me, "Mommy, Daddy *only* speaks one language." That was her *Sleeping Beauty* book moment. As babies, it's just words and sounds and communication. Then we begin to understand that there is a labeling and a compartmentalization that is language. The brain just flows from one language to the next and, of course, may occasionally experience a glitch.

※

I struggled with an eating disorder for about twenty years. I began dieting when I was five and finally developed a healthy relationship with food around age twenty-five. In between were horrible bouts of bulimia, very restrictive eating, low weight, heartburn, health problems, and retreating from friends. I knew that what I was doing and how I was eating made no sense. I knew how harmful my behavior toward my body was. I could have a completely logical conversation with a therapist on a couch about the ins and outs of eating disorders. But then I would go home and live in a seemingly endless cycle of restricting and vomiting. I would get so frustrated with myself: Why couldn't I just fix this?

I kept hoping that I could figure it out and have a happier life than the one I was leading. I used to think, *This cannot be my destiny. I need to make my life better.* Though I sank to extreme lows, somehow I always returned to a place of determination. And I am like this to this day. We must always remember that our dark moments are just moments, and with hope, curiosity, and problem-solving, there is a chance to find the light.

There's still so much confusion surrounding eating disorders and what causes them. People assume that girls who have them just want to be thin and that society is toxic, pushing women to be skinny and bombarding them with unattainable standards of beauty. This may be true, but it's also important to understand that eating disorders don't just affect girls and can result from a number of factors, not just societal pressure to look a certain way. I was told so many times that my eating disorder was caused by vanity that I eventually began to believe it. This association is something I hope we can move beyond. An eating disorder often runs deeper than a desire to be thin. Mine certainly did. Separating myself from the idea that my eating disorder was about thinness was what ultimately liberated me.

My husband, who has OCD, and I, who recovered from an eating disorder, both attempted to soothe our intrusive thoughts by doing things that could be masked as "good." Eating disorders can often be passed off as being conscientious about food: You're careful about what goes into your body. Your eating habits are "healthy"! Someone with OCD can pass as being "clean"—specific, organized, and structured.

I asked my husband recently, "What if I told you what *you* think is clean and organized doesn't seem clean and organized to anyone else?" I had realized this about myself years ago when I was battling my eating disorder: it was probably crystal clear to others that what I was trying to pass off as healthy behavior was far from it.

We all see our lives and our paths through the lens of our experiences and gained knowledge. Becoming a mother and breastfeeding allowed me to see how our relationship with food is intense from day one. Babies are born with the need for nourishment, screaming until they get milk. The act of eating almost immediately calms a baby . . . and this is how we begin our lives.

How did I heal my eating disorder? I will attempt to explain, with the very important caveat that there is no manual for it. (I go into this in depth in my first book, *The Living Clearly Method*.) If it had been solely about food, I could have been locked up and forced to eat a certain set of meals at certain times and instructed to exercise in specific ways. However, for me, it wasn't about eating: food was something to obsess about, a distraction from the real root of my pain and dysregulation.

It's hard to learn how to connect with our internal systems. We live in a world that encourages disconnection from ourselves. From the time we're very small, we're told: *Don't be sad; be sad; don't be tired; be tired; be hungry; stop asking for a snack; be sorry; don't be loud; don't bother them; speak up but don't say that.* We all do it with our kids, and we have all had it done to

Dominic Neitz

us. This is not a call for raising kids without rules. We live in a culture where we must work together and be decent human beings. But we need to relearn how to connect with ourselves, because our disconnect is causing tremendous harm.

I found my way to reconnecting with myself through yoga, somatic experiencing (a type of therapy that focuses on the nervous system), determination, and, most importantly, the desire to take care of myself. I was introduced to yoga at around the age of twenty.

For the most part, I have been given the freedom to teach from my heart and my soul, passing knowledge on to my students and learning just as much from them—perhaps more than I could impart at times. I felt like a vessel: able to absorb knowledge from so many and then hand it out to others in need. I knew I was struggling, and I also knew I was in a place where I could heal, even if that place was far from perfect.

It is through movement, breath, and awareness that we can teach communication between the body and mind, therefore allowing for regulation within our dysregulated systems. If we are happy, if we are in love, we get a certain sensation; the same if we are stressed, sad, tired. The issue is that some of us have become dissociated from the average feeling our body emits. This is why we go to extremes to get dopamine hits and find ourselves falling into toxic patterns . . . because at least we are feeling, right? We have become desensitized to the most beautiful parts of our lives, which are the ones we think of as filler. Think about your body as you are reading this book: How many sensations are being generated at this very moment?

Where are your hands on the pages? Are your legs touching each other or a surface? Where are your feet? How is your tongue placed in your mouth? How fast is your heartbeat? We experience so many sensations that go unnoticed until an extreme one comes about. Imagine, as you are absorbing these ideas, that a loud sound goes off and you startle. What does your heart do? Your blood pressure? Then imagine that what startled you was easily recognizable as something safe—maybe a car door being slammed. Now imagine your fright instinct beginning to settle and going back to a place where you no longer notice those sensations of simply being. Is it mundane? No! All these seemingly mundane moments are what add up to your life. Once I realized this, I didn't want to let them pass me by.

In the classes that I teach, we have periods where we move very quickly and periods where we are as still as we can be.

We are never completely still as long as we are alive. Our heart beats, our instinct to swallow persists, our breath is moving. There are millions of micromovements that we are always making. Yoga fascinates me because in the course of a session we alternate between intensity and calm, feel a wide range of sensations, then try to continue to reconnect with our bodies off the mat. It's like learning how to touch-type. In the beginning, we have to think about where the letters are, maybe even peek. Then eventually we can look at the screen and make words, then sentences, then thoughts begin to pour out of our hands, just as I am doing right now as I type this. The practice of noticing sensations then naturally seeps into our daily lives.

Little by little we become conscious of small sensations and eventually begin to truly feel everything. Does my relationship make me happy? My job? Where I live? How I'm eating? How I'm living? I learned that it isn't necessarily being in a yoga pose that is important; it is how I intentionally get into it and how I intentionally get out of it. These processes are just as important as the result.

The mind, then, is the bossy part of this balance, and it often misguides us. While the body speaks the language of movement and feeling, the mind's language is chatty and gets easily distracted or spirals in the wrong direction. The mind mainly focuses on the past and the future, but rarely on the present. The mind ignores the body until the body experiences an extreme sensation. The physical practice of yoga allows us to open a pathway of language and understanding between these two parts of ourselves. The only time we are truly present is when we are focusing on the sensations the body is feeling at this very moment. If I think about the past, my body will react to my thoughts. If I think about the future, my body will have a physical reaction to those thoughts. It is through leaning into the sensations of here and now—and focusing the mind on them—that we can truly live in each moment. It takes tremendous practice, which we must always continue to work on. But, just like touch-typing, it becomes easier, and the gift is that it enhances many of life's best moments.

For two decades I tried everything to rid myself of my eating disorder. I went on different diets, weighing food, weighing myself, chewing my food way too many times (it's gross), telling myself I was worthy, stupid, a lost cause . . . I tried it all. There was so much trial and error, along with tears, health scares, angst, hope, and determination that finally got me to the moment when I realized what I had to do in order to have a healthy relationship with food.

When I was twenty-four, in an attempt to help me, my brother flew to New York City and took me to a nutritionist. The nutritionist was expensive, he was far away, he gave me so much paperwork to fill out, and he was a complete jerk. I barely remember anything from the visit, but I do remember him saying I didn't know what was good for me, that I was misguided, and that I was basically dumb. I flipped out (though I'm sure I excused myself in a decent way, because I am terrified of being perceived as rude). But on the car ride home after the visit, I went into a cuss-filled tirade about how I was sick and tired of devoting so much of my life to this. I got so mad . . . and then suddenly it felt clear to me. Wide-eyed, I declared to my brother, who was looking at me like I'd just lost my mind: "I know what I have to do: I have to *feel* when I am hungry, *feel* when I am full, eat and *feel* it in the moment, and eat what I *feel* I want."

I had gotten so wrapped up in the shoulds and shouldn'ts and all the manuals on how to have a good relationship with food that I'd lost myself. That was my tipping moment. And I did it. Was it all smooth sailing? No. But for the most part I started *experiencing* the act of eating rather than thinking about it so much. The feeling became my guide and my faith and comfort. We are designed to eat, and food is designed to taste good, and this is a good thing. I wasn't broken, and there was nothing inherently wrong with me. It was the work I'd done to connect my mind and body that allowed me to regulate my nervous system and therefore simplify the act of eating instead of complicating it.

I cannot tell anyone the right foods for them to eat, or how much, or when. These are distractions and are often used by people to create diets that they can monetize. I don't promote any particular eating habits, although I prefer a mostly plant-based diet myself. This is what feels best for me and how I've decided to feed my children. They know that as they grow they can make different choices but that I'm raising them this way because it makes sense for us right now.

My eating disorder wasn't about being thin, about being accepted, or even about food. It was a storm I had created and continued to live with because I was dealing with dysregula-tion. By understanding my system, reconnecting with myself, and working on my ADHD, I was able to regulate myself enough to change my behavior and nurture myself properly in a way that felt and tasted good.

Someone recommended I read the book *Waking the Tiger* by Peter Levine. This book changed my life, because it taught me about the concept of the nervous system and trauma. So-matic experiencing gave me some excellent tools to guide me in my yoga practice and reconnect with my body, thereby healing my eating disorder. It is these tools—and determination and hope for living a less internally tortured life—that allow me now to have a great relationship with food.

While I would prefer never to have had an eating disorder, I am so grateful for what I have learned from it. I carry the lessons with me in the way I manage my nervous system in different situations. It has not always gone easily and there have been difficult moments, but I'll always be proud that I overcame something that once seemed so impossible.

7

MY PEOPLE

Friendship comes in so many different shapes and sizes. We speak to some friends every day who are by our sides through anything; then there are those we see occasionally whom we enjoy or who make us laugh, and those we mostly interact with on social media. When it comes to friendships, I try to meet people where they are and not come in with judgments or expectations. By treating each person as an individual, meeting from our own authentic selves, we can form a strong bond.

While it may not be evident on the outside, inside I often squirm in social situations where I don't know people well. Obviously my ADHD doesn't help with the fidgeting, the challenge of concentrating on what people are saying, interrupting, talking over people, and blurting things out. As much as I crave belonging and acceptance, I often get in my own way and then obsess about it afterward.

New York is the kind of city where everybody is from everywhere. I came for school. Some people come for a specific career, to be an actor or an artist, to be in business or work on Wall Street, or to just experience the city's energy. It's one big melting pot, and I think that people who thrive in New York City derive comfort and belonging from living in this kind of chaotic mix.

For example, I've found that people who don't fit into a box often gravitate to others like themselves. Most of my friends are multilingual and from many different places and haven't really taken a conventional path. We are a mix of things and know that belonging isn't just about speaking one language or enjoying a certain kind of music or eating a particular food.

Alec told me that Marlon Brando once told him during a meeting, "Humans are like dogs: sniffing each other out." The nice thing for me about meeting somebody else multilingual is I don't have to explain myself. We're always trying to categorize people: *Where are you from? What language do you speak? Where did you go to school?* By categorizing people, we're trying to understand them.

When you don't fit into a box and have been repeatedly asked getting-to-know-you questions by people trying to size you up, it's a relief to find other un-boxable people. We get to bypass all the primitive thinking and dive right down to the soul. I choose to find joy and positivity in the fact that I resist categorization. It's been quite a painful road to get here, but I can safely say that I have arrived and no one can oust me from this place.

There are moments in life when you realize how much of a product of your family you are. As we become adults, we try to detach ourselves from our roots to some extent in order to find our independence. We see our children do it; it's normal. Ultimately, our job is to go off and live our own lives.

And then there are times when I look at my life, and realize, *Of course I'm like this. It's because my family is so much like this.*

My close family lives in Europe, and so I have a chosen family here in New York. I tell my children that these friends are their aunts and uncles and cousins. I actually have mixed feelings about the term "chosen family," because children don't choose how they're raised; they're born into it—whether that's what language they speak, what religion they practice, or who they consider family. It's decided by their parents.

And I grew up exactly the same way: my parents chose people, and my grandparents chose people, and my great-grandparents chose people. And this has made up our family for many generations. There is just as much love, belonging, and connection in a community like this as there is in one related by blood. I know this because I have both in my family, and it is all that I have known. I spent all my important moments with them: birthdays, holidays, long dinners where the kids fall asleep under the table, occasionally tying knots in the adults' shoelaces first. I was that child. These are my childhood memories. There have been times—only as a public figure— when people have questioned my family structure and my family dynamic. The pain I felt when I had to defend it or explain it is something I never want to endure again. I never had to before I met Alec. I didn't choose to be raised this way, but I love it and I'm proud of it and I'm passing that way of life on to my children. It's all that I know.

I take strength from my grandfather, who was adopted by his father and knew of complicated belonging too well. He

always encouraged me to embrace who I am and taught me how our family is very worldly. Those who find a problem with this have blinders on from some predisposed notion of how things are "supposed to be." My grandfather taught me to allow myself to be molded and changed by my surroundings. Flexible and curious people can live life to such a full extent.

One time, when Carmen was small, a woman tried to tell her that her uncle, a dear friend of mine, wasn't her "real" uncle. For some reason she felt the need to explain to a child what was "real" family and what wasn't. Nonconfrontational me, at that point I didn't get angry, but privately I was very upset by it. It undermined my own feeling of family stability and who I consider to be a loved one. When I was a little girl, before I'd go to sleep, my mother would have me list the people who loved me. It was such a sweet thing. And we'd include everyone in our family community. That's how I grew up and that's now how I'm raising my own children: in this tradition that I love. We don't focus on blood; we focus on love.

Recently we were up in Vermont, and Alec took the four older kids out with two of my best friends—a gay married couple—and I took the three little ones with the babysitter to a local farm.

There's a breakfast spot there that we love. It feels like you're stepping back in time: everything is so fresh and delicious. It's family operated and it's the best. That day I went in there to get food for the kids while they waited in the car with the babysitter. Alec had been in there before with our four older ones. There are often these local men who sit at the far end,

and they're always discussing politics and farming and just living their lives in the community.

Even though I always say hello to them, I doubt they remember me each time. That day, I ordered sandwiches from a waitress whom I'd never seen before, and then she went over to the two guys to take their order, and I heard them talking about Alec. It was only the four of us in this small shop, so everything was loud and clear. And one of the guys went, "He comes in here with his twenty-seven nannies and his kids . . ." In general, just being pretty snarky about my family. The waitress was kind of excited to have something like this to talk about, so she chatted with him and they both kept harping on the nannies and calling my family "weird."

I turned to them and said, "I just want you to know that you're talking about my husband and my children, and those weren't nannies; they are my friends. My family doesn't live in this country and Alec's parents have died and a lot of his family lives far away. And so we've made our friends our family. And I want you to know that this is who you're talking about." I was embarrassed because I could have just stayed silent and waited for our sandwiches.

They also got embarrassed, and the man said, "I wasn't saying anything derogatory about him!"

You would think that I would have stopped the awkward interaction, but alas I continued: "I know you're very nice. I always see you and we love the people and the food here, and we're grateful to be here. We do have wonderful nannies who work with us and they're also like family, but those two particular men are not our nannies. They are here spending time with us. And they are two people. Not twenty-seven."

And . . . I continued further: "We come here from New York because everybody's really kind, and we'd like to find a community here."

One of the men said, "Well, I just leave your husband alone when he comes in."

"He doesn't want to be left alone," I said. "He wants to have a community here. When we come in, we'd love to be part of things, to connect and have a good experience."

My sandwiches were done at that point, so I thanked them for the delicious food and told them I hoped to see them all again soon.

And my inner monologue shoved me out the door, chastising me the whole way.

※

An acquaintance texted me recently and asked me about my health. She said she'd heard that I was gravely ill. Stunned, I replied, *"I am in great health, to the best of my knowledge."* Then I asked where she'd heard this from. She replied that she couldn't tell me who had told her because she needed to protect this woman. Knowing that I couldn't avoid her, I decided to respond. I texted her back, *"Well, you can tell them I am definitely sick of gossip! Sometimes we protect the wrong people. Just be wary, people who spread lies and gossip about other people often do it to everyone. Protect yourself. If you ever find it in your heart to tell me who I need to be careful of, I would appreciate it. My family has been through a lot and I want to keep my distance from people who would want to hurt me. We have been through too much already to have to deal with any unnecessary negativity."* I'm fed up and too tired at this point to tolerate toxicity. I knew I'd evolved when I was able to act instead of just going off and obsessing about it. I wasn't being mean or cruel and I didn't block this woman. I just created an immediate boundary: this is my life; this is my health.

We're very spiritual in my family. And so, when somebody says something about my health, it sparks a fear in me that that person is wishing me ill. The tremendous power I have in going up against this is to not allow it to filter in or feed more energy into it. Ultimately, I have to stop obsessing. Stop processing. Stop asking questions. Stop trying to make something rational out of something that is just plain mean and irrational. And I'm trying to do that with all the toxic things in my life.

There are moments when people have real power over me, and this creates real effects. It could be something to do with a job, or my kids, or my reputation. But a lot of the toxicity is tied up in how my mind won't stop turning it over, instead going around and around it. The work now becomes focusing on switching gears and putting my perspective on something that is more positive. Once I do that, the situation can fade away and these people will have less power over me.

One of the schools that I went to when I was growing up was an international school with a modular system, which meant you could go to different places during different parts of the year. It was socially divided into the international students and the local American students. Though I was born here in the United States, I fit in more with the international community because of how my brother and I were raised. I also lived very far from the school—my commute was an hour and a half each way on public transportation.

Like many teens, I went through phases while at this school and didn't have a lot of close friends. Instead, I had the kinds of acquaintances who were pleasant with me during the day, but then I would leave school and not interact with them. There were two girls who I would eat lunch with, and one of them was from Taiwan. Her name was Sandie. We didn't hang out outside of school, but she was so nice, and it was a comfort to have someone to sit with at lunch and not eat alone. After school ended, we moved on and completely lost touch.

One of my best friends, Danny, whom I met right after I married Alec, went to a design school. And, small world, it turned out that Sandie went to the same school with him! When she realized the connection, she asked Danny to put us in touch. At a time when I was feeling so sad, she wrote me the sweetest messages, which truly saved my life.

Here are some highlights from our exchanges:

> **Sandie:** *Hi, Hilaria! You've been on my mind lately with all the news about where you're from. I think it's so ridiculous and I can't believe how mean people and the media have been to you. To me . . . you've been the same person all along, and have stayed true to who you are. You are such a beautiful person, always have been, keep on doing you . . .*

> **Hilaria:** *I'm so grateful for this message. It means the world . . . I am the same person.*

> **Sandie:** *And you've always been multicultural, since the first day I met you!*

Hilaria: *I am always happy when I hear from people who remember that about me. I feel like I've been gaslit.*

Sandie: *It was never a secret. I've thought so many times about commenting on posts, but felt like that won't do anything, because people just want something to be nasty about . . .*

Hilaria: *I think as we get older, we get more comfortable with ourselves. Parts I used to separate, I don't anymore.*

Sandie: *Absolutely! The older I am, the more in touch with my Taiwanese side I am, whereas in high school and college I think I was trying to assimilate more to being "American" . . .*

Hilaria: *I appreciate it. It's a hard situation because people who actually know me and care for me didn't speak to the press . . . But then only the trolls are heard.*

It went on like this, each of us catching up with an old friend, and finding comfort in telling each other, "I'm that way too." We laughed about the fact that I speak only two languages and she speaks five; you can imagine how many words she forgets and the languages she mixes up all the time.

Those who reach out to us in our darkest times are beautiful souls. I was so grateful to have someone say to me, *You're not crazy. This is who you are and this is how you've always been.* Even though I knew that, sometimes outside noise makes you lose yourself. Sandie helped me find my way back.

That was quite a few years ago. Sandie and I still exchange texts, and recently, when she was visiting New York, we got to see each other. It had been more than twenty years! I was so grateful to her for being kind to me during a hard time, reaching out to me when she didn't have to. We have similar feelings about belonging. We get each other without having to explain. Who knew that my lunch buddy would help save my mind and my life and help restore my sense of self?

When I was preparing to join Alec at his trial in Santa Fe, and struggling to decide which of our children to bring, my dear friend Yoel offered to come with me. There was only one nonstop flight to Santa Fe and it was scheduled for very early in the morning, around 1:00 a.m. There were moments when I was like, *I can't get on this plane. I don't know what to do.* Alec needed me there to support him, but my children at home also needed me. They were aware that something was wrong, and I wanted them to stay in their routine, to have some sense of normalcy.

Yoel helped me through it all. He took care of me, he took

care of Carmen and Ilaria, and he helped us get through this difficult time. During the day, when I was at court, Yoel was with the two kids, taking them to fun activities, giving them too many treats, and spoiling them. They call him their uncle. There is no better friend than one who takes care of you by taking care of your family. Because of Yoel, I could be there for my husband in his time of need. I feel very lucky to have that kind of friend in our lives, a person who can make you smile even when you think you'll never smile again.

8

WHERE DO WE GO FROM HERE?

As women, we can be fierce, the best defenders, the warmest nurturers. Our friendships with one another are deep and we can laugh our way through wild shenanigans. We can also guide each other and support each other through our hardest times with wisdom that we learn along the way and from each other.

Do you ever feel like you are too much and not enough? There is a toxic system that is set up to keep us striving for perfection. It's like: Be perfect but don't show that you are; do it effortlessly but tell everyone that you are one giant mess. There is no winning here.

I hope you are taking notes, because you are probably just as confused and exhausted as I am. As women, it is assumed that we are required to do this balancing act where we run through an impossible obstacle course, ducking opinions and leaping over societal rules. We are expected to do this without complaining or breaking a sweat—and, most importantly, to never question the system. I am sick of the "good-girl" mentality that has been drilled into so many of us: believing our value and self-worth are determined by external validation rather than who we are; striving for unattainable perfection; putting others' needs ahead of our own.

These rules are all made up. We aren't property, and no one can own our sense of self-worth and shame us into submission, despite harsh opinions and unsolicited advice and the ridiculous notion that things have to be done in one particular way.

How many times, as women, do we feel responsible for trying to make sense out of something that is just someone else's toxicity? I'm working on this practice of stopping and taking a breath when I get upset about something that is said about me, remembering: That's someone else's garbage! It's not mine and it has nothing to do with me. They pretend that it does. Everyone is entitled to their opinions, but we are also entitled to not let those opinions into our lives, and to protect our inner peace. It's not our job to manage how other people are feeling, manage their misinterpretations, manage their love and their anger. We don't have to absorb people's bad energy—or pass it on—because it is just too much for our bodies to keep contained and festering inside us.

Gossip exists within communities, schools, families, and, yes, the tabloids. We can't stop it. But we can work on developing a filter for what we allow in to preserve our mental health and happiness.

It is this filter that will give us the freedom and the courage to lead our lives our own way. Because we all know that life throws curveballs, things go haywire, and each child comes out as their own person with brand-new tricks up their sleeves. As mothers we have to pivot, figure it out, pivot, figure it out, each time in a completely different direction! There is no one right way. Any negativity only serves as a distraction and needs to be swept away.

This is going to be about practice—and never perfection. And much of it begins with refusing to direct negativity toward other women. These past few years I have found myself responding more and more to gossip about other women with (a) "Who cares? I hope that she is living her best life"; (b) "Good for her! I wish her well"; or (c) my very favorite: "It's none of my business." I encourage you to try it. It's disarming and totally knocks people off guard. They are expecting a reaction, and when you don't engage and give them one, you've defused the situation and prevented any kind of escalation and additional bad feelings. While we each want the freedom to live our own rightful way and should give respect to other women who also deserve this, none of this means that we have to live exhausted, alone, and putting up walls around us, attempting to figure it out by ourselves. Sharing and hearing from other women and mothers about what works and doesn't work has always been a guiding light for me and many others. But please keep in mind that there is a major difference between telling someone what to do and sharing what works for you, and being supportive and inclusive. That's what this book is about.

For fourteen years, since that fateful day when the press called me, outing me for dating Alec, people have been telling me who I am and who my family is. Every single opinion, good and bad, has been people speaking about me and for me. From now on, every project I do will be about me speaking for myself.

Recently, I had an experience where I realized I hadn't grown—or healed—as much as I thought I had. I was sure when I began writing this book and looking back at my own life that I'd reached a place of strength—the kind of strength I admire in women who hold their heads up high, who talk about how they've overcome adversity, how they've pushed on and refused to let anyone knock them down. This was the proud impression I had of myself after turning forty: I thought I walked among them—until I had this experience that triggered my fight-or-flight response and sent me into a tailspin. And I let it happen, which saddened me. I let myself down.

I lapsed into days of tears and sleepless nights, my old habit of concocting imaginary situations in the shower when I would make up my best responses to any troll behavior. I failed.

I don't want to close myself off when hard things happen

anymore. I know this happens to some people, and that's understandable and okay, but it's not how I want to live. It feels cathartic when I show who I really am, that I have found my voice. I don't want to be torn apart for clickbait. I don't want anyone to do that to me again. I am not bait. I am a whole human being.

Like the women I admire so much, I want to set an example of how to move forward with my head held high. It hurts when people say unkind things about me and my family. It hurts when people are mean to me for no reason. I would be lying if I said that it doesn't, or that I have gotten used to it, or that I can somehow just block it out. It's normal to be hurt, because we are human beings who want approval and to understand when things don't make sense. Cruelty makes no sense—plain and simple.

We all know that people who've been hurt often hurt others, but I try to be an example of the opposite truth: that people who've been hurt also heal others through their desire to not have one other person experience the pain they did. I tell my children that when they're hurt, even if they have done something wrong, it is an opportunity for them to choose whether they want to grow into a person who lifts others up, or someone who tears others down. Pain and love are interconnected. We feel love because we know pain, and we feel pain when love is absent or withheld from us. Toxicity poisons the giver first of all, and it is our choice whether we allow that poison in.

The best I can do is to practice positivity—to not let negativity take root and claim too much power over me. I lean into the good and into good communities. I speak up about toxic systems and painful experiences because I don't want other people to be treated badly. It is also a practiced reminder for me to keep toward the positive. I am learning how to reframe things and let them go. I do that because I want to be a good example for my kids and a good mother to them, a good partner to Alec, and a good friend and daughter and sister. And I also do it for myself because I love life, I love joy, and I want to be happy. That is something we all deserve.

I'm inspired by people who stand up for themselves and those who have the courage to stand up for others. That might be the countless brave people who talk candidly about their mental health, or those who try to rise above labels society pins on them. People who know that we're much more than just one simple thing and that the simplicity of belonging is what unites us all. That's where I choose to be.

I'm not going to get it right all the time and I definitely didn't get it right during this recent experience, but I'm going to continue to try my best, learn, and evolve, and forgive myself when I get it wrong.

I was talking with one of my girlfriends recently, and she remarked that I had been thrown into a metaphorical fire by the entertainment media and didn't feel I had permission to step out of it. She wisely told me that this next chapter in my life is about finding my voice and having autonomy and agency. Even though I want to be likable and easygoing, and I want to be fun and a good sport, I can't give away any of myself or my agency.

I am who I am, I am proud of who I am, and I am proud of how we are raising our children. I will no longer serve as an example of women having to play the same game by different rules.

I was looking up quotes about female strength and there were so many by incredibly inspiring women. Almost all of them had to do with the struggle, and being misinterpreted, and knowing who you are, and finding your community. And so, it hit me: If we are all feeling such pain and having to toughen up so much, can't we just skip to the good part? Can't we just stop? Just let us be—unapologetically be.

I hope this book will remind you that there is no one right way to do anything, that the judgments, the shoulds and shouldn'ts, are all just noise. We can be welcoming and warm and know our limits and also be aware that the manual is NOT included but we don't have to figure it out alone. We can use our voices and find our courage to be ourselves. Brush away the negativity as calmly as we can, because it never had anything to do with us anyway.

I am here for you, even if we never meet in person. The energy of human friendship is powerful and far-reaching. I can tap into it and feel good energy from afar. The more we have conversations about this and refuse to give ourselves away, the stronger we will become.

Through the years, I've experienced so much growth. But I'm still human and I'm going to get scared and mess up and struggle sometimes. I can't prohibit people from speaking for me, gossiping, and telling my story, but I can tell my own story, as I've done in these pages, and I hope it is me that is ultimately listened to. I'm going to live my life as freely and as happily as I can. And I'm cheering you on in the hope that you will do the same.

RonShoots

ACKNOWLEDGMENTS

This book was written over the course of a time in my life that had much positivity but also so much uncertainty and fear. Life throws the good and the bad at us, and having a community who came to me and wanted to encourage me to tell my story and just be human has helped me so much.

I am eternally grateful to Jen Bergstrom, Aimée Bell, Pamela Cannon, Jill Siegel, Sophie Normil, Caroline Pallotta, Nancy Tonik, John Vairo, Karla Schweer, Tom Spain, and the amazing Hanna Preston.

Thank you to Emma Rosenblum, who has guided me and knows how I think, and who can rein me in and let me fly.

Thank you to Jill Taratunio, who is my anchor. I love you so much.

Thank you to Emily Jones, who made me laugh when writing a book was so hard. We came up with so many book titles, like *They Are Giving Book Deals Away to Anyone These Days* and *Same Shit, Different Woman*.

To my friends and family, Alec and my children: thank you for being supportive, and I love you.

ABOUT THE AUTHOR

Hilaria Baldwin is a wellness and fitness expert. She was previously the cohost of *Mom Brain*, a weekly podcast about parenting, which consistently ranked in the top ten in its category. She is the author of *The Living Clearly Method: 5 Principles for a Fit Body, Healthy Mind & Joyful Life* and cofounder of Yoga Vida in New York City, where she lives with her husband, Alec, and their seven children. The family is currently starring in the new TLC series *The Baldwins*.